DASHIELL HAMMETT

A Daughter Remembers

AN OTTO PENZLER BOOK

DASHIELL HAMMETT

A Daughter Remembers

JO HAMMETT

Edited by Richard Layman with Julie M. Rivett

CARROLL & GRAF PUBLISHERS . NEW YORK

DASHIELL HAMMETT
A DAUGHTER REMEMBERS

Carroll & Graf Publishers
A Division of Avalon Publishing Group Inc.
161 William St., 16th Floor
New York, NY 10038

Library of Congress Cataloging-in-Publication Data is available.

ISBN: 0-7867-0892-1

Book design by Debbie Glasserman
Printed in the United States of America
Distributed by Publishers Group West

For Mama

PATRONS ARE REQUESTED TO FAVOR THE COMPANY BY CRITICISM AND SUGGESTION CONCERNING ITS SERVICE   1201-8

WESTERN UNION

CLASS OF SERVICE

This is a full-rate Telegram or Cablegram unless its deferred character is indicated by a suitable sign above or preceding the address.

NEWCOMB CARLTON, PRESIDENT   J. C. WILLEVER, FIRST VICE-PRESIDENT

SIGNS
DL = Day Letter
NM = Night Message
NL = Night Letter
LCO = Deferred Cable
NLT = Cable Night Letter
WLT = Week-End Letter

The filing time as shown in the date line on full-rate telegrams and day letters, and the time of receipt at destination as shown on all messages, is STANDARD TIME.
Received at 9509 Santa Monica Blvd., Beverly Hills, Calif.   Phone OXford 4709 1931 APR 2 PM 6 26

SAL246 23=VN SANFRANCISCO CALIF 2 559P

MISS JOSEPHINE HAMMETT=

184 NORTH CRESCENT DRIVE BEVERLYHILLS CALIF=

I STILL THINK YOU ARE A PAIN IN THE NECK DONT LET THE

RABBITS BITE YOU LOVE AND A KICK IN THE PANTS=

DASH.

THE QUICKEST, SUREST AND SAFEST WAY TO SEND MONEY IS BY TELEGRAPH OR CABLE

Papa sent me this telegram in April 1931. I was not yet five.

FOREWORD

FOREWORD

After Poe, Dashiell Hammett is probably the best-known crime writer in America. He pioneered a literary form—hard-boiled detective fiction—and at least two of his novels, *The Maltese Falcon* and *The Glass Key*, achieve what he called "the absolute distinction of real art." When he fell short of that high standard, Hammett still wrote enduring crime fiction.

Hammett was self-educated. At the age of fourteen he dropped out of high school after one semester to help support his family, took a job with the Pinkerton's National Detective Service in 1915 as soon as he was twenty-one, and worked as a detective until poor health forced him to quit six years later. He began writing in 1922 to support his new wife and child, supplementing the disability income he drew as the result of respiratory illness he first suffered while in the army during World War I. Within a dozen years he was so successful as a novelist that he did not have to write fiction for money any longer. And he didn't.

In those dozen productive years, Hammett taught himself to write stories that seemed, as he put it in another context, "real as a dime." Using his experience as a detective for material, Hammett created realistic characters and placed them in settings and plot situations he knew to occur. He developed a nameless fictional detective he called the Continental Op who became the most popular hard-boiled detective of the 1920s. Then he set about drawing on his extensive reading in history, philosophy, literature, and science to create fiction that did more that tell an entertaining, believable story with accurate description. It addressed problems basic to the human condition.

Hammett wrote five novels—*Red Harvest* (1929), *The Dain Curse* (1929), *The Maltese Falcon* (1930), *The Glass Key* (1931), and *The Thin Man* (1934). Most readers agree that the first two, which were conceived as a set of related stories, are prototypes for a new kind of writing that is tough, realistic, unsympathetic, knowing, and engaging. He was compared with Ernest Hemingway, who began writing fiction at the same time as Hammett and who, in large part, shared his worldview. For his next two novels Hammett set the standard higher. He wanted distinction as a novelist, not a hard-boiled mystery novelist, and he succeeded.

By the time *The Glass Key* was published, Hammett was a national celebrity. In the course of the year 1930 he went from being barely able to support his family to earning more than he could spend. Hollywood was where the money was in those early days of the Great Depression, and Hammett focused his attention there. He wrote one more novel, *The Thin Man*, which was his most successful in terms of earning power and his least satisfying as a serious work of literature. By the time that last novel was published, Hammett was regarded as one of the hottest writers in Hollywood, and he remained so for half-a-dozen years until the Hollywood vices—women, alcohol, and self-indulgence—took their toll and brought him to a hospital bed again.

His recovery came in stages. First, he found purpose in political action. A Marxist, he began working for social causes he believed in. Then he entered the army during World War II, where the order of military life helped stabilize him. After the war he renewed his political commitment while maintaining his interest in literature—which now included the theater and movies, as well as his fiction, which he no longer was able to complete to his satisfaction.

In the early days of the Cold War just after World War II, when the alliance between the United States and Russia dissolved and membership in the Communist Party came to be considered a crime, Hammett was ever more vocal in defense of civil rights. In 1951, he was called to testify before a federal court regarding his political activities, and he chose to remain silent. The penalty was six months in jail and the blacklist, which not only cut off his income but brought the scrutiny of the IRS, which found that Hammett owed more than he could hope to repay. He lived modestly the last decade of his life, supported by his veteran's pension.

Hammett's personal life was as unorthodox as his writing career. His health forced him to live separately from his family after 1926, when Jo Hammett, his younger daughter, was born and he suffered a relapse of tuberculosis. He had recovered by the time his novels were being written, but by then he knew that family life was not for him. In 1931 he met Lillian Hellman, who became his steadiest companion for the rest of his life.

Despite his celebrity, Hammett was an intensely private man, difficult to read, and hard to know. Until his *Selected Letters* were finally published in 2001, he was among the most mysterious of American writers. Four full-length biographies shed only partial light on him. What was known about Hammett came from his works, from the scant documentary evidence available, from brief reports of those who knew him, usually late in his life, and from the official profile painted by Lillian Hellman that aimed to provide a dreamlike fictional image without particular reference to fact.

In this memoir Jo Hammett provides the fullest personal portrait of her father ever written.

There is a lot of Dashiell Hammett in his daughter Jo. She is reserved, as he must have been except when he was drinking. She is confident in her own opinions and content to let others think as they will without judging them unduly, a quality that characterized her father. She is introspective like him. She is catholic in her interests, as her father notably was, though he would have parted company with her when the word got capitalized. She is straightforward and patient for the most part, as he was, though she shares his impatience with dopes. And, once she makes up her mind, she is as stubborn as her father. An important clue to understanding what he was like comes from knowing her.

She came to this book reluctantly and yet deliberately. Her father died in 1961, when she was thirty-three. She and her children were, by all evidence, among his chief interests in the last decade of his life. After she grew up and graduated from UCLA, he looked upon her as the most responsible of the Hammett women. Yet after his death Jo, along with her older sister Mary and their mother, was all but disenfranchised by Hammett's longtime companion Lillian Hellman, who was executrix of his will.

Hammett always had an unconventional relationship with his family. Jo only lived with her father briefly, but he maintained steady contact with her, Mary, and their mother. He wrote them regularly, visited when he could, and supported them until the last years of his life, when his money and energy ran out.

After 1931, Hammett lived with Lillian Hellman, when he wasn't living alone. Though they never married, they were devoted companions, and Hellman exerted the authority of Hammett's wife. While she deferred to Hammett with regard to his family while he was alive, after his death she largely ignored them. She never met Hammett's wife, Jose. She knew Mary well from the years after World War II when Mary lived in New York with and around her father, struggling with mental illness complicated by drug and alcohol abuse. She was acquainted with Jo, met her children, and expressed admiration for the stability of her life—a quality not normally associated with Hammetts. When Hammett died, Hellman felt it her right, as well as her duty, to take control of his estate and to shape his literary legacy.

Lillian Hellman was a controller. She gained control of Hammett's copyrights in a complex legal maneuver, then proceeded to shape his posthumous reputation with a lover's jealousy. She created for him the image of a benign, inscrutable recluse, happy to live the last thirty years of his life in her shadow. She wrote about Hammett herself, and when other biographers began showing interest in him as a subject, she appointed an authorized biographer who would tell his story as she would have it—though the authorized biographer had a mind of her own. She instructed her friends and associates to refuse contact with researchers seeking information about Hammett, and she instructed the Hammett family to speak to no one about him without her approval. On December 29, 1975 she wrote to Mary Hammett, "I have every intention of trying to stop various projects about your father, and if you or your mother in any form collaborate it will, of course, defeat the possibility of stopping them." They complied.

Jo had her own family to raise, her own life to live, and while Lillian Hellman was alive, Jo was content to defer to her authority. Hellman sought, however, to control Hammett for all time. She died in 1984, leaving instructions in her will about how Hammett's copyrights should be administered. She left the income from all of Hammett's works to his daughters, but she added a Hellmanesque qualification that eloquently expressed her condescending attitude toward them. Implying that Jo was not competent to handle her father's estate, though she was named as alternate executrix in his will, Hellman established a Literary Property Trust to control Hammett's copyrights and appointed three trustees, who were her own fiduciaries. It was not a workable arrangement.

At length, with the assistance of her son, Evan, who is an attorney, and the support of her three daughters—Ann, an employment development specialist for the State of California; Lynn, an economist specializing in energy issues; and Julie, associate-editor of *Selected Letters of Dashiell Hammett*, Jo gained control of her father's novels and permission of the trustees to compile an edition of his letters. This book began as contextual notes for Hammett's correspondence with his family, but it soon became clear to those of us involved in the editing of that book that Jo's memories of her father deserved separate publication.

The text of this volume was conceived as a collection of unconnected memories—recollections that came to Jo as she read family letters or leafed through her photo album. As these vignettes accumulated, they came to form a narrative—what Jo knew of her father's life, and how he affected her, Mary, and her mother. Photographs are an important element of the memory Jo has of her father, and they are an integral part of this book. Hammett was an avid amateur photographer, and the family carefully saved the photos he took while he was with them. Many have captions in his hand. Most of the photos are from the family album, though the earliest snapshots of Hammett come from his relatives in Baltimore. Occasionally a photo from a source outside the family is used, but only when it is needed to complement the text.

No one knows Dashiell Hammett as well as his daughter. She writes with the unmatchable authority of experience. This memoir begins to set the record straight by presenting a loving but unembellished profile of Jo Hammett's father. It is a family portrait.

RICHARD LAYMAN

25 MAY 2001

PREFACE

PREFACE

There have been perhaps half-a-dozen biographies of my father. Of these I've read three cover-to-cover, leafed through two of the others, and closed one after two pages. I grew up a habitual reader of biographies, awed by the mountain of work they entail and enjoying the illusion they provide of intimacy with another life and time. Reading those that deal with my father, however, has not always been a happy experience. It has changed the way I read all biography and the way I trust what I read. It has made me skeptical and acutely aware of the role that motive, historical judgment, and discretion play in their creation. Biographers seem to me to be subject to an impressive array of temptations:

Of not discounting obvious impediments: resentment, malice, loyalty, unreliable witnesses, or plain bad memory.

Of assuming the natural superiority of the living over the dead.

Of deciding that a life is to be judged by its last days.

Of insisting that those who prefer the shadows will be flattered by the spotlight.

Of presuming that a life can be caught and pinned up on a page for later examination.

Of preferring sensation over substance.

You can't libel the dead, the courts have ruled, and they can make no defense. Or perhaps their silence is their final defense. "Silence, exile, cunning," James Joyce's advice to the living, may work as well as any for the dead.

Brooding on this, I find my thoughts turn quite lethal, and on a dark night, in a black Irish funk, I think bad cess to them all: the shooters of fish in a barrel, the scholars and the tale bearers—ex-maids and butlers, body-guards, summer help, analysts, and best friends—the diarists and mem-oirists—wives, widows, and children. They are eaters of the dead, myself included.

Morning comes however and paranoia fades, and I know all general-izations are false: Some attorneys are honorable; some biographers are objective, or try to be: some are aware of their own limitations and walk softly over the graves of the dead. For those we ought to be grateful. Their work is a useful and necessary evil, and we ought to honor it. Still, it might be helpful if biographers, before they sit down to write, consider their own mortality and what may come after.

ASSEMBLING THESE PIECES for publication has not lessened my doubts about biography. I note how untrustworthy I have been as a witness, how my perceptions and loyalties have shifted over the years. Children are eas-ily seduced by the glamorous, the extravagant, the seemingly stronger par-ent. Disneyland Daddy wins hands down over the Stay-at-Home Mommy. And I was as susceptible as any other child—lost in admiration for my mysterious father, undervaluing Mother's quiet virtues. When I was old enough to judge the limitations of her life, instead of being sympathetic, I was irritated by what I thought of as her lack of spunk. Lillian Hellman (my father's long-time companion) was clever enough to encourage this, and I was flattered enough to let her. It wasn't until I had children and grandchildren of my own that I recognized my mother's grit and integrity. I came to see that her life had been as much an exercise in courage as my father's. I saw that what my parents had in common was a singular bravery—a persistent cheerfulness in the face of despair.

So I make my poor excuses (always leave yourself an out, Papa once told me) for what is recorded here. It is not a biography. It is what the title says: what I remember—impressions that are imperfect, imprecise, biased, maybe even poorly interpreted. It is not true. But it is as true as I can make it.

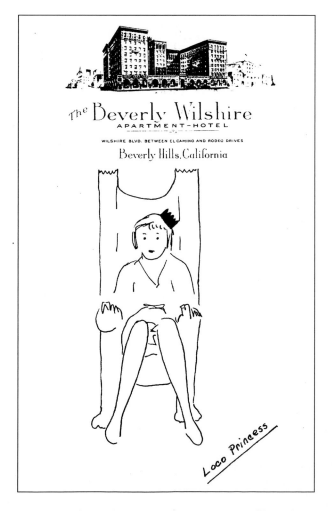

Papa drew this caricature in about 1937. Loco Princess was one of his nicknames for me.

My father at about nine months. He was a large baby, weighing in at eleven pounds.

The graveyard in St. Mary's County is thick with Hammetts. Favored names on the markers repeat themselves over and over: Anne, Rebecca, Julia, Steven, Richard, Samuel. It was, and still is, a place where family history matters. The first Hammetts had come from England in the sixteen hundreds, put down roots and, mostly, stayed put. They were small farmers, tobacco growers, shopkeepers. There were Hammett-labeled canned goods. Hammetts fought in the Revolution and the Civil War. A Union prisoner-of-war camp, with a reputation as terrible as Andersonville's, occupied the southern tip of the peninsula. The Civil War, over less than thirty years when my father was born, had been a bitter time for these people whose land was occupied by Northern troops but whose sympathies lay with the South.

St. Mary's County was a Tom Sawyer kind of place to grow up. It is isolated on three sides by the Potomac and Patuxent Rivers and Chesapeake Bay. There were streams, ponds, and woods teeming with game. When my father talked about his boyhood that was the part he remembered—summers on the farm when the boys could take their shoes off, playing in the woods with his brother, fishing and hunting. That was what stayed with him all his life—the love of the outdoors.

Below are photos from the Baltimore Hammett family album of Hopewell and Aim, the Hammett family farm, where my father was born. My grandparents lived there with my great-grandfather and his second family in a three-story farmhouse. His first wife, Ann Rebecca, had been a first cousin. She died in the late 1880s, and at the age of fifty he married again, this time a much younger woman. The pictures shown here of the house where my father was born shown here is from a photo taken in the 1970s. The addition on the right was made well after Papa was born, and when he lived there the house was unpainted.

He also brought from there a certain and unshakable sense of who he was—a Hammett, an American, and, although Maryland was a border state, more of a Southerner than not. His parents were often in dire straits financially, and his father was considered the family ne'er-do-well, working unsuccessfully at several trades, but Papa grew up knowing that he had come from people who were firmly rooted in American history.

When I first saw a picture of Hopewell and Aim, the Hammett farm, I felt a pang of envy for what he discarded so lightly—the beauty of the land, the identity of the extended family. Those are things my sister and I missed growing up hopscotching around Southern California, living in rented houses, playing in parks or small back yards, with no cousins to visit, no big family Christmases to look forward to.

Children, of course, make do with what they have, and what we had was the Pacific Ocean to splash in, plenty of neighborhood kids to play with, good public libraries. We had Mama, who was always there, and Papa who was in and out, exciting and scary mysterious, as he still is in my mind.

YEARS LATER WHEN Lillian mentioned that she and my father had thought about having a child, I was less than thrilled. Oh great, the kid would have French nannies, private schools, and skiing vacations in the Alps, I thought, mixing this phantom child up in my head with Scottie Fitzgerald, whom I secretly envied. In my mind I dressed Lillian's child in some of the elaborate outfits I'd seen Scottie pictured in—the silk appliqued Christmas dress, the English riding clothes, the fur coat and cloche hat that I particularly coveted. She appeared solid enough in them, but when I tried to put Lillian in the picture—reading her stories, making cocoa, rubbing her legs with Balm Ben Gay—my imagination failed. Seeing Lillian as a mother was beyond my power.

...

She stared at her glass while saying, "He's my father. I never liked him. I never liked Mamma." She looked up at me. "I don't like Gilbert." Gilbert was her brother.

"Don't let that worry you. Lots of people don't like their relatives."

EXCHANGE BETWEEN DOROTHY WYNANT AND NICK CHARLES,
THE THIN MAN, CHAPTER 4

FOR DOROTHY WYNANT in *The Thin Man*, and most of my father's characters, family life was no bed of roses. In *Red Harvest*, Elihu Willsson's manipulations get his son killed. In *The Glass Key*, the father is his son's murderer. I don't pretend to know how Papa came to such a dim view of family life. Once when I was ten or eleven, he accused me of being ashamed of my parents. Then not waiting for an answer, he went on to say that it was okay; everyone was ashamed of his parents. When he was little, he said, he liked to imagine that he was adopted, and one stormy night his "real" father would come driving down the road to reclaim him. He didn't go on to explain what this "real" father would be like, but I imagined he would be very different from the one he already had.

Although he seldom mentioned him, it was clear to me they were not close. Richard Hammett was, by all accounts, a sharp dresser, a drinker, and a womanizer. He had been so during Papa's boyhood and remained so for the rest of his life. Papa complained to my sister in the forties that he wished his father would quit bragging about his lady friends. Though Annie Hammett had been dead for many years, it still rankled Papa to be reminded how his father's affairs had hurt her.

Richard was hardly a doting grandfather. Once in the twenties, Mother recalled, when Papa was very ill and we were in desperate need of money, Papa wrote asking for a loan and was refused. That was something, though he never mentioned it, that Papa would have found hard to forget.

Still, I saw a spark of admiration once in the forties when Papa wrote that his father had lost a leg, to diabetes I think, but was feeling better and had started rumba lessons. Papa always liked the extravagant gesture. When his father was in his last days, Papa sent money and clothes, but he did not deliver them himself.

Of all the family, he felt closest to his mother. Annie Bond Dashiell came from a family that had been in America as long as the Hammetts. They were French Huguenots who had fled during the time of the religious wars, immigrating first to Scotland and then, in 1653, to Virginia. "De

I studied pictures like this one of Scottie Fitzgerald with her parents in papers and magazines and envied her globe-trotting lifestyle and inexhaustible wardrobe. If my father and Lillian had a child, I imagined she would be like Scottie, the center of a golden world, lavished with clothes and unimagined advantages. I didn't want to dislike this phantom child, but I couldn't help it.

This is the only photograph I know of my grandparents, Annie and Richard Hammett. It must have been taken in Baltimore, where they moved in 1901. My father is on the left beside his younger brother, Dick, and older sister, Reba. Papa looks to be about fourteen, which was about the time he quit school. Dick would be twelve and Reba fifteen.

Chiel" became Dashiell along the way. They carried exalted memories and certain pretensions with them. In Maryland an early Dashiell will prescribes an ear mark for the livestock: "Cropt on right ear with a flower delure on the left with a slit." The family records describe a chateau near Lyon; a coat of arms ("A shield of gold with a band of red; and a label of three pendants, over all in chief,"); and a motto—"Neither soon nor late"—which my father commented was about as worthless a bit of advice as you could come up with.

Annie held herself a step above the roughhewn Hammetts and, I think, encouraged her elder son to do so as well. It was his mother who gave Papa the sense that he was someone special who would make his mark in the world.

When Richard left St. Mary's County to seek his fortune and failed, the

Reba, Dick, and my father at the Stricker Street house in Baltimore, where they lived with my grandmother's mother. Papa is the taller boy. They attended Public School 72, and Papa made up his mind to read all the books in the public library.

Papa, about age eleven, with a pet rabbit.

Papa with Dick and Reba in the backyard on Stricker Street. By the way they are dressed, I think they must be celebrating some special occasion. Maybe it's Reba's birthday. She looks about sixteen to me. Her baptismal name was Aronia Rebecca.

Dick and Reba in about 1910. Papa was fond of Reba, and she was a devoted aunt to Mary and me, sending us hand-sewn dolls and little stone crosses.

family moved to Baltimore, where they lived with Annie's mother. Annie was an energetic woman, who went out as a nurse to supplement the feckless Richard's earnings, a situation Papa deeply resented, perhaps thinking she lowered herself. But Annie herself was not strong—there was a persistent cough that might have signaled tuberculosis. It is possible my father was exposed to that disease early in his childhood.

MOTHER WAS BORN in Basin, Montana, in February 1897, the eldest child of Margaret and Hubert Dolan. The exact date is uncertain. She was probably born at home. There was no birth certificate and when, as an adult, she finally got her baptismal certificate, the year and day on it were not what she expected. She was christened "Josephine Annis Dolan."

Hubert Dolan was a miner whose family had come from West Virginia—I presume the men worked the coal mines there. Margaret—known as Maggie—had come over from Ireland as a girl of sixteen. Her grave marker shows that she was ten years younger than her husband.

My grandmother was twenty-seven when she died in 1901. She left three children: Mama, three and a half; Walter, two; and a baby boy, Eddie. Maggie's death must have been a terrible blow to Hubert. He had to work and cope with three small children. To complicate matters, he drank. I imagine the children being passed around among friends and neighbors in the dirt-poor mining village, and I imagine my mother trying to comfort her little brothers. All her life she loved babies and taking care of them. Little Eddie was finally taken in by relatives in Butte, where he died before his first birthday. Within three years after Maggie's death, Hubert was gone, too. An unmarked hollow lies between Maggie's and Hubert's graves, where I think the baby must rest.

After Hubert's death, Mother and Walter went into a Catholic orphan-

Mother, in the sailor blouse, on the lawn of the Kelly's house with her cousins in Anaconda, Montana. Mother appears to be about twelve.

This is Basin, Montana, southwest of Helena, where my mother was born. Her father worked in the mine there. Both of Mama's parents were dead before she was six, and she spent a year in a nearby Catholic orphanage before going to the Kellys.

This is the Kelly house in Anaconda where my mother grew up. She was taken in by her paternal aunt after her parents died. Capt. William Kelly had a good job with the Anaconda Copper Company.

age in Helena and stayed for a year or more. It was the start of her lifelong distrust of nuns (which would be reinforced later when she took nurse's training in a Catholic hospital). She was down scrubbing floors at the age of seven. She recalled being locked in the coal cellar for some trifling sin. Hubert's sister, Alice Kelly, had a house full of kids herself and, I suppose, wasn't in a hurry to take in any more. But one night Maggie appeared to her in a dream and pleaded with her to take Josephine out of the orphanage. She went next day and brought Mother to her home in Anaconda. The Kelly's were comfortably middle-class. Her husband, "Captain" William Kelly, had a good job with the Anaconda Copper Company in Butte. Mother lived with the Kellys until she was fifteen.

The Anaconda years were not happy ones for Mama. Mrs. Kelly eventually had a dozen or more children. I remember her as a querulous, sickly old woman always complaining of drafts and her sciatica. Mother understood and sympathized: Any woman with that many kids had reason to be querulous. Alice Kelly had wanted to do her duty, but she hadn't the time

Here are the cemetery and the graves of my mother's parents, near Helena. Maggie came from Ireland when she was sixteen. Hubert's family was from West Virginia. They both died young, leaving three small children. An unmarked hollow lies between their graves, where I believe Eddie, Mama's baby brother, was buried.

or energy to spare for another child. And Mama always felt like the orphan. She got a new dress when the girl nearest in age got one, so the neighbors wouldn't talk. But it wasn't all bad. The night Mama moved in (she must have been seven) she took the toddler of the family, who had been displaced by the new baby, into her bed. She cuddled and cared for him as if he were her own. This was the closest relationship she would form there.

Mama got through the eighth grade in Anaconda. That was considered

Mother and her younger brother Walter making their first communion in about 1907. Walter grew up and married, but he died in his thirties. When I was born Walter sent my parents $50, a generous gift in 1926.

My mother at about fifteen. She quit school after the eighth grade. That was considered plenty of education for a girl.

plenty of education for a girl. Then at fifteen she went into nurse's training at St. James Nursing School in Butte. I don't think nursing held any great appeal for her, but her options were limited. Staying longer with the Kellys was not one of them. She spent three hard years at St. James. The nuns were tough cookies. She went to classes in the morning and worked with patients in the afternoon. Then, as likely as not, she was assigned to private duty at night and sometimes got no sleep at all. But she got through it and graduated with a degree as a registered nurse. In pictures of Mother in her nurse's uniform, I see a stranger—a pretty, confident young woman

This is Mother's graduation class from the nursing school at St. James Hospital in Butte. She is at the far left in the front row. She was fifteen when she entered the three-year course. After that she did private-duty nursing.

Miss J. Dolan, R. N.

TELEPHONE 738-W

Mother was proud to have gotten her diploma and to be earning her way as a registered nurse. She had business cards printed up, giving her telephone number in the nurse's quarters.

who had survived a Dickensian childhood and the harsh training of nursing school. She looks competent, relaxed; she's good at what she does. "To the little nurse everyone likes," a postcard from a patient reads. Patients would have felt easy with her. She was cheerful, considerate. She had cards with her name printed up and went to work in the hospital.

1917 was a turbulent year in Butte. A disastrous explosion in the Spectator Mine killed over a hundred men; there were violent strikes by the miners; IWW leader Frank Little was assassinated. The United States entered World War I. Mother and some of her nursing friends joined up, happy to become Army nurses, serve their country, get out of Butte and see the world.

. . .

I had a little bird and his name was Enza.
I opened up the window, and in-flu-enza

CHILDREN'S SKIPPING RHYME

IT WAS 1918. The war in Europe was coming to a climax. Our troops were coming home, bringing with them a deadly virus, one that would ultimately kill five-hundred thousand Americans and radically transform my father's life.

Papa was twenty-four when he enlisted in the army. He had been a wage-earner since he was thirteen. The family fortunes were low, and as the eldest son, he'd dropped out of high school and gone to work for the Baltimore and Ohio Railway as a "call boy" (office boy). That was followed by a string of short-lived jobs, which lasted until 1915 when he saw an ad in the paper for the Pinkerton's National Detective Service.

Pinkerton's was the premier American detective agency. They had done heroic service for the government in guarding public officials and protecting against espionage. They had also solved some spectacular crimes in the private sector, but they were best known for their brutal strike-breaking activities. Their unblinking eye with the caption "We Never Sleep" was a familiar logo.

Papa was trained under a crusty operative, James Wright, who would become the model for the Continental Op in his *Black Mask* stories. From Wright he absorbed the basics of private investigation, as well as a personal code of honor that would stay with him the rest of his life.

He left Pinkerton's in June of 1918 to join the army. Sent to Camp Mead, Maryland, for basic training, he was eventually assigned to the ambulance company there. The Spanish Influenza struck first and hardest at East Coast army camps. The ambulance company personnel at Camp Mead, whose job it was to transport the sick and wounded, would have

My father in the backyard on Stricker Street in 1918 in civvies and in his World War I uniform. He was an operative for the Pinkerton's National Detective Service before he joined the army that June.

My father's ambulance company during World War I. He is fifth from the right in the back row. Camp Mead, about fifteen miles from Baltimore, was a receiving center for troops returning from Europe. They brought with them the deadly Spanish Influenza virus. My father fell ill with it in October 1918 and was in and out of the hospital until his discharge.

This photo from my mother's album is a mystery. Papa went back to work for Pinkerton's in the Northwest after he was discharged. This might be a picture of a Pinkerton's work crew, possibly strikebreakers. Papa is standing fifth from left in the back row.

been directly exposed to the virus, which, perversely, was most often fatal to the young and vigorous.

In October Papa came down with flu-like symptoms—fever, cough, and weakness. The doctors called it bronchopneumonia. He got better, then worse; better, then much worse. Discharged in May with the diagnosis of untreatable tuberculosis, he was as much disabled as if he had been gassed in the Marne.

At home in Baltimore his health was erratic. He worked sporadically then landed back in the hospital. In May of 1920, perhaps in desperation, thinking that a big change might somehow help, he moved across the country to Washington and went to work for the Pinkerton's office in Spokane.

His work there took him all over the Northwest and eventually to Butte, Montana, where the mine owners were locked in a bloody struggle with the radical Industrial Workers of the World. He used what he saw there in his first full-length novel, *Red Harvest.*

But still his health would not hold, and in the fall of 1920 he was admitted to the Cushman Institute, a Public Health Service Hospital at Tacoma, Washington. It was at this point that my parents' lives converged. Mother had spent the war years working at various army hospitals across the Southwest. She came to Cushman with the rank of second lieutenant. Papa had been discharged as a sergeant. The disparity in rank does not seem to have been a problem. They met and fell head-over-heels in love.

NEITHER OF MY parents talked much about their time at Cushman. When my father did, it was to mention some prank they had got up to—like throwing pie tins over the partition into the part of the ward where the shell-shocked guys slept. My mother only seemed to remember how strict the older nurses had been and how rough some of the men were.

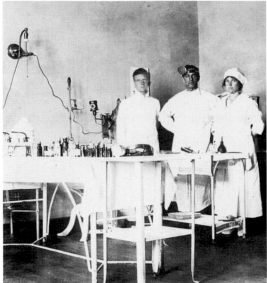

Mother standing at the door of one of the buildings at the Cushman Institute in Tacoma, Washington. In 1920 the unused Cushman School for Pallyup Indians was converted to a United States Public Health Service Hospital. The patients were veterans with respiratory illness or shell shock. Initially, a staff of four medical officers and seven nurses cared for about 200 patients. Above right and below are photos of the operating room and a patients' ward.

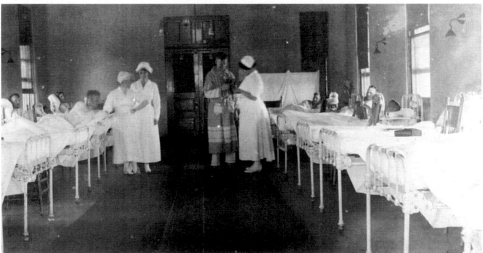

It wasn't until after my sister's death in 1992, seventy years later, that I got a glimpse of their meeting, of how things had been between them for those few months in Washington in the winter of 1920.

Mary died after some months in a nursing home. Her troubled marriage to Kenny Miller had ended well before that. Neither Kenny nor Mary had been competent to manage their business affairs, and Kenny's brother, Wally Miller, and his wife, Bonnie, generously stepped in to help out. The house in west L.A., which Papa had bought Mother was to be rented.

Both Mary and Kenny had been pack rats. They threw nothing away. The house and garage were crammed tight with broken furniture, tools, boxes of clothing, magazines, books. The Millers plowed through this ocean of stuff and called me to say that they had found some things of my mother's and Mary's that I might want.

It was a while before I actually got around to claiming what became known in the family as the "Miller hoard." Partly this was due to practical considerations. But mainly it was because of the vague uneasiness I felt. For

Patients and staff at Cushman Institute outside one of the wards. Papa is third from right in the second row, sitting next to Mother. She had outranked him in the Army, when she was a second lieutenant and he had been an enlisted man.

Mother, right, in back of an ambulance holding up her end of a stretcher. This photo was probably taken on the grounds at Cushman Institute, where my parents fell in love.

reasons I still don't understand, I was reluctant to dig up any more relics of the past.

During this time I began, with my friend Don Herron's help, to organize my father's letters for publication. Don kept insistently urging me to see what the Millers had found. So, at long last, arrangements were made and my daughter Ann and I drove up to the Pacific Palisades home of Wally Miller. We brought back half-a-dozen cardboard boxes and a small trunk. It didn't look like much—Mary's old underwear, we joked driving home. Boy, were we ever wrong. I called Don in San Francisco that evening. "We have bonanza!" There were photo albums, Hammett books, business papers, family mementos, a set of corrected galley proofs of *The Dain Curse*. And there were about a hundred and fifty letters from my father to Mary. Eventually we would retrieve even more of these. Mary, it turned out, had been the dutiful daughter, keeping and protecting almost everything he had ever written her.

In May 2000 my mother's garage was getting another, final, cleaning out. Kenny had died, and the house on Purdue was being sold. More Hammett material surfaced. Again with a daughter, this time Julie, I made the trip to the Miller's home. We retrieved another box, a suitcase, and an ancient hatbox. I recognized some of the things in the boxes, but the hatbox contents were new to me: pictures, postcards, souvenirs, and a dozen letters written in green ink. Their dates ran from February 1921 to June of that year. My father, who had been hospitalized at the Cushman Institute in Tacoma, Washington, had been sent south to the drier climate of Camp Kearney in Southern California. He was writing to my mother, who was still on the nursing staff at Cushman.

Reading these letters was a strange experience. First of all, it was hard for me to think of my father as ever being that young—and that open hearted. He sounds for all the world like the young guys I danced with Saturday nights at the Santa Monica USO in the forties. They were lonely and scared under their tough-talking fronts. They fell in love easily, looking for something to hold on to, a girl to come home to. They were full of sweet talk and the same kind of gentle teasing Papa used. They wrote letters just as ardent and sometimes as awkward as his. It's only when you come upon a special turn of phrase—"I deserve all the love you can spare me! And I want a lot more than I deserve"—that a hint of the-writer-to-be slips out.

My parents' romance didn't last long. They were together for less than eight years, but it's nice to be reminded that they started out as sweet and romantic, as playful and loving, as any couple anywhere. It is the letters that didn't survive however—the unheard part of the dialogue—that are the more poignant for me. These imagined letters from my mother are as real to me as those I can hold in my hand. Taken together with his, they tell the story of their courtship. He's the pursuer. She enjoys being pursued, takes her time answering him, puts off sending him a picture. She writes

My mother, father, and an unidentified nurse, referred to in my family as the chaperone. This photo must have been taken in winter 1920-1921 in Tacoma, Washington.

motherly advice about eating right and "taking the cure," by which she meant not drinking.

She was cautious and rightly so. As charming as Papa was, he was no great catch: He had no education or trade; he was an avowed atheist; he gambled and drank; and he was in very, very bad health. He might even have been tubercular, though she didn't let herself believe that. Tuberculosis was a whispered word back then and very often a death sentence.

Set against those minuses were the plusses. He was funny and smart. He had a quality she couldn't have put a name to, but it was there, something about him that set him apart from the other men. And he loved her, with "All the love north of Hell." That was more love than she'd ever been offered before. Still she was wary.

In spring 1921, the tone of her letters changed: She wasn't feeling well. She was cranky, got into spats with people, cried easily. Not like the sunny Miss Dolan at all. Any woman reading those letters would have guessed in a moment what was wrong. But he didn't think of it. He was a man; he didn't have to. She put off telling him, kept hoping it was something else, that she'd wake up and find it was a dream. She told nobody. She wouldn't write it down, because if you wrote something down or said it out loud, then it was real. But by the middle of June it was too real to be denied.

The Green Ink Letters end with the one Papa wrote from Spokane on June 2. He's been discharged and talked vaguely of going east. "I haven't any sort of plans for the future but I reckon things will work out in some

In my aunt Reba's album this photo of my father is identified as having been taken near San Diego. In February 1921 he was transferred to Camp Kearney, another USPHS hospital. Its drier southern California climate was thought to be better for respiratory patients.

The food, served by two Filipino boys, was good. There was not much conversation and none of it was religious. It wasn't so bad.

THE OP IN *THE DAIN CURSE*, CHAPTER NINE

Religion, Papa said, was supposed to bring families together, but what it usually did was set them at each other's throats. The Hammetts had a Catholic background. Although the Dashiells, his mother's side, were Episcopalian, they were so high-church that it didn't bother her to switch over when she married.

My father seems to have been a natural born skeptic. As a boy, he and his pals would sit at Mass and substitute "Hurray for us" for the "Pray for us" in the responsory. He generally poked gentle fun at all things religious. Of course, it would have been strange if he hadn't. Intellectuals of his day were, with few exceptions, atheists or at least agnostics. It didn't bother me much. I remember thinking, "Well, he's right about everything else. Just this one thing he's got wrong."

But he never made a big deal out of it, or tried to convert anyone. In San Francisco he stayed with us while my mother went to Mass. In New York in 1941 he gave me taxi fare, and I went alone to St. Patrick's—my sister having long ago left the church.

His ideas about religion, as about everything else, seemed to reflect a quiet certainty. I don't know if he was as absolutely assured as he appeared and wouldn't have known how to find out.

manner." And they did, with Mama writing to him that she was pregnant. And him writing back: It's okay, come to San Francisco and we'll get married. I'll take care of you.

Mama didn't save that letter; it was too painful. This wasn't the way she'd wanted it. She was terribly ashamed, of course, but another part of her was hopeful. She loved him; she'd told him so. And he loved her. And there was a baby on the way; she'd always been crazy about babies. It might turn out to be what she'd always wanted, a family of her own.

The "what if's" abound. What if Mama hadn't gotten pregnant? What if they hadn't gotten married? What if Papa hadn't been too sick for anything but writing? What if he'd picked a city other than San Francisco to settle in? Would there have been the *Black Mask* stories, the Continental Op, Sam Spade or *The Maltese Falcon*? Or me, for that matter? There are no answers. Blind chance strikes in all kinds of ways. Sometimes it's a bacillus, and sometimes it's a baby.

MAMA TOOK THE train to San Francisco in July 1921 and stayed in the room Papa had booked for her at the Golden West Hotel. They were married on the seventh of that month in the rectory of Saint Mary's Cathedral. She was surprised to learn that he had been raised Catholic. I suppose the subject of religion hadn't come up much before then.

They moved into the Crawford Apartments at 620 Eddy Street. They were to stay at that address, in two different apartments at different times, longer than anywhere else in San Francisco. When Papa began writing, he worked nights in the kitchen and days, when he was well enough, at the public library. There was a flat roof that served as a playroom and setting for many of our early photos.

Papa had a small disability pension, but with a wife and baby on the

My parents were married in the rectory of St. Mary's Cathedral in San Francisco on July 7, 1921. Mother was surprised to learn that Papa was a Catholic.

way he needed more than that. He put up an "Employment Wanted" sign in a shoe repair store on Market Street. When that didn't pan out, he went back to work for Pinkerton's. But his lung problems came back with a vengeance, and in December 1921 he was out of work again.

Mary was born October 16 of that year. She came home from the hospital a long skinny baby, carrot-yellow with jaundice but grew into a pretty child with fine blonde hair—Papa called her the Tow Head—and Mother's clear blue eyes.

As is the case with most first-borns, Mary had lots of pictures taken of her. She is always well dressed and posed with impressive toys—stuffed animals, dolls, and a jumbo-sized elephant—too expensive to have been anything but gifts. In these early pictures she is sometimes smiling. She very rarely smiled in later ones.

You can usually tell who the photographer was. In Mother's shots heads

In early pictures of my mother I see a woman I never knew. A young woman in a fancy hat and satin dress on the San Francisco roof with a toddler. I wonder where she is going. To Mass? No. She's too dressed up. Somewhere with my father? I doubt it. I never heard her say, "We used to go eat at ___'s," or "We went to visit the ___" Maybe her Montana relatives were in town and she was going to show them around. Would she have gotten that dressed up for them? I don't know.

are frequently cut off or lower limbs amputated. Papa's shots are well composed. Also he had a camera that let you write the subject and date on the negative. His printing is neat and accurate. Mother writes "Baby 9 months" on the back of her snapshots, leaving you to wonder what baby.

Papa began a course at Munson's Business College for newspaper reporters, dropped out, and then started writing advertising copy on a freelance basis. He liked the writing and began to send out fiction pieces to magazines. In October 1922 *The Smart Set* published his first story, "The Parthian Shot." The pay was laughable, but he was on his way.

He put more and more of his time and energy into writing and sold to several different magazines. His style was gradually changing from the sort of pseudo-sophisticated stuff *The Smart Set* used to what it would become: realistic and quietly ironic. He became a regular for the pulp magazine *Black Mask*. The first Continental Op story, "Arson Plus," appeared there in October 1923. He had found his niche.

Mary began school in San Francisco at Charing Cross kindergarten. A cab picked her up every morning, which must have been an expense. She

After they were married, my parents lived at the Crawford Apartments, 620 Eddy Street. These photos of them were all taken on the roof there. It was like an outdoor living room for them and Mary, who was born in October 1921.

Papa in San Francisco in October 1925. His Continental OP was a favorite with the *Black Mask* crowd.

This photo is captioned on the negative in my father's hand "Mary Jane bathes 6.15.22."

Below: Mary was eight when she wrote her name on the last page of *The Dain Curse* galleys. Papa's second novel was published in the fall of 1929 just a few months before the family split up. Papa went to New York, and Mama and us to Southern California, where Mary continued a lifelong habit of writing her name on every found object—first editions, the Daily Missal, dictionaries, and encyclopedias.

learned to print in a neat boxy hand and practiced writing "Mary Jane Hammett" in crayon on any piece of paper she could find—on books and letters and on the last page of a *Dain Curse* galley proof. Papa played with her, drew little stick-figure pictures, and read to her. But he was strict, too. He returned the circus tickets he bought when she misbehaved. Mary wrote a note to Mother afterwards: "Mama i will be good a good girl. And the Baby to. And papa will be a good boy. The End." Mama saved it along with Mary's embroidered baby shoes.

I was born in May 1926, three days before my father's thirty-second

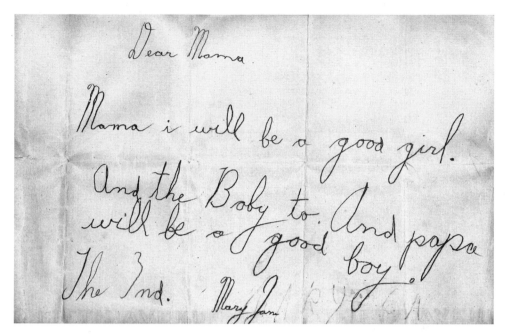

Dear Mama.

Mama i will be a good girl.
And the Baby to. And papa
will be a good boy!
The 2nd.   Mary Jane

Mother saved this note from Mary, along with her baby shoes. I doubt she ever looked at it in later years—I hope not anyway, because the irony would have been pretty hard to take. None of Mary's predictions were close to coming true. Even the Baby, which was my name until my teens when I finally rebelled, failed to meet expectations.

birthday. Papa had gone to work for Samuels Jewelers as advertising manager a few months before. It was his first well-paying job and gave him the kind of recognition he needed. But in July he fell ill again.

My mother said my father seldom drank in the San Francisco days. She blamed the sales meetings he had to attend when he was in advertising for getting him started. Mother was always one to shift blame away from the family when she could. But she saw, correctly, that he was a shy person and needed the confidence of the bottle for business and social occasions.

In the summer of 1926 my father was very sick. Alone in his apartment he waited to die. He was so weak that he arranged chairs across the living room so he could get to the kitchen and bath. My mother took us on a long visit to her Montana relatives. He didn't die, and we came back to San Francisco, but the Public Health Service nurses feared that we children would be infected, so they made us move apart. On my first birthday we were living across the bay in Fairfax. My father came over Sundays on the ferry and spent the day.

He kept a separate apartment even after we moved back into the city—people have suggested that he liked the freedom that gave him for poker parties or to entertain women. The latter is more likely, but I think that he just needed the peace and privacy to write and to be alone. My father was a man who always loved and needed solitude.

My mother came to accept the necessity of their living apart, but she never considered them to be "separated." From the tone of his letters at that time, I don't think he did either. Legal separation or divorce was a

On the back of this photo, my mother wrote, "Papa in a kitchen in San Francisco." It looks like Mother's photography; she often cut off heads or feet.

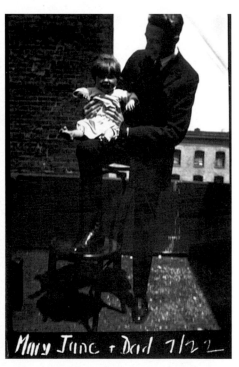

Mary June + Dad 7/22

Papa with Mary on the roof at the Crawford apartments. His handwriting on this negative is meticulous. He was very neat and economical in everything he did; there was no wasted motion.

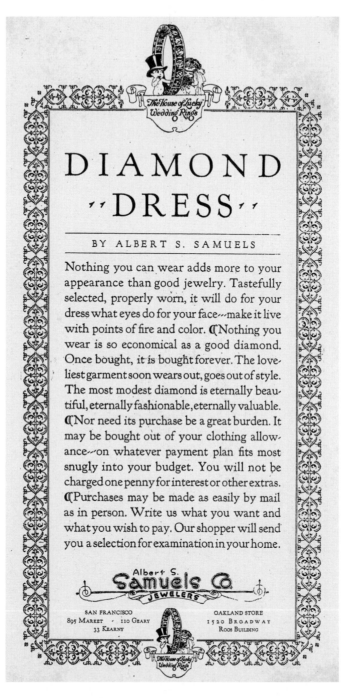

The House of Lucky Wedding Rings

DIAMOND ''DRESS''

BY ALBERT S. SAMUELS

Nothing you can wear adds more to your appearance than good jewelry. Tastefully selected, properly worn, it will do for your dress what eyes do for your face—make it live with points of fire and color. ❡Nothing you wear is so economical as a good diamond. Once bought, it is bought forever. The loveliest garment soon wears out, goes out of style. The most modest diamond is eternally beautiful, eternally fashionable, eternally valuable. ❡Nor need its purchase be a great burden. It may be bought out of your clothing allowance—on whatever payment plan fits most snugly into your budget. You will not be charged one penny for interest or other extras. ❡Purchases may be made as easily by mail as in person. Write us what you want and what you wish to pay. Our shopper will send you a selection for examination in your home.

Albert S. Samuels Co JEWELERS

SAN FRANCISCO
895 MARKET · 110 GEARY
33 KEARNY

OAKLAND STORE
1520 BROADWAY
ROOS BUILDING

Mama saved this proof of an ad from Samuels Jewelry Store, so it is probably one Papa wrote. The language sounds quaint today, but I think it represented a part of my father that most people don't see: his love of really good, expensive things in classic style. He was very selective in what he wore; his shoes were the best; his tailoring, impeccable. Cuff links and watches had to be elegant and, of course, expensive. If you gave him anything that didn't meet his standards, he accepted it with sincere thanks and gave it away.

This picture of Mother, me, and Mary was taken in Anaconda, Montana in fall 1926. Papa's TB had gone contagious, and Mama had to get Mary and me away from him. I was baptized while we were there (which must have shocked the Kellys, because you're supposed to do it right away), and Mary saw her first snowfall.

My father in an early twenties photo. He was so thin one health worker said he looked like a famine victim. At the best of times he was a light eater; at the worst, he seemed not to eat at all. But he was a drinker. When it wasn't alcohol, it was coffee, orange juice, or milk.

disgrace in my mother's eyes, and she bravely put up a front: Yes, they were temporarily living apart, but it was only because of his work, his special requirements.

It was a long gradual transition from that stance to admitting that their marriage was over. He had told her once that "she should take care of the children and he would take care of her." She held on to those words as long as she could, and he did too. His support checks might be late, but we never doubted they would come. Nor did we doubt that he loved us and thought of us as his family, even if living together as a family was not a possibility.

In pictures from the San Francisco days my mother looks thin and worn out. Her days were a rush to get us up and out to the park in the morning, home for lunch and naps at noon, and back to the park in the afternoon. Her social life was with the mothers and children she met at the park—visits to the beach, Fleischacker Zoo, donkey rides in Golden Gate Park. There was always worry about money and my father's health.

Papa helped as much as he could—sometimes made bread or lemon pies, stayed with us so Mother could go to Mass or the matinees she loved. He played with us—soaped the mirror and drew pictures on it, made shadow animals on the walls, crafted a little paste-up book for me of poems and pictures.

Both my sister and I disliked our given names, Mary Jane with good reason, I thought. It would be hard to imagine one less suited to her after

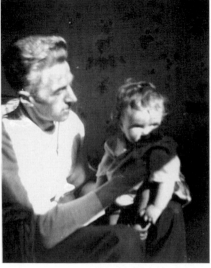

These snapshots were taken across the bay from San Francisco in Marin County, where Mama got a little house after we came back from Montana. Mary was six. I had my first birthday and learned to walk over there. Papa was well enough to go back to work at Samuels and continued writing for *Black Mask*. He would come over on the ferry Sundays to see us.

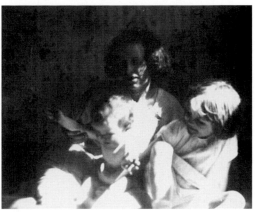

Mother looks thin and worn out in these pictures. She had a lot to worry about—money; Papa's health; keeping Mary and me fed, clean, and dressed; and, now that they were living apart, how the future would play out.

she grew up. The "Jane" was eventually dropped for just "Mary." But there was nothing more that could be done with that. When I complained of my unwieldy given names—"Josephine Rebecca" seemed an unnecessary burden on a child who struggled with penmanship and spelling—Papa disclaimed any responsibility. Mother was in charge of the name department he said, and she'd picked both of ours.

In time "Josephine" was shortened to "Jo" which had pleasant echoes of *Little Women.* But I still held some grievance against my father for not using his literary and parental authority to give me a classier sounding name. If I had been asked I would have chosen "Margaret," the name of all my dolls and my maternal grandmother's name, though I didn't know it then. I can't imagine what he would have chosen.

Sometime in the forties my father mentioned wistfully to me that I was supposed to have been a boy. It's hard to believe with his health and their

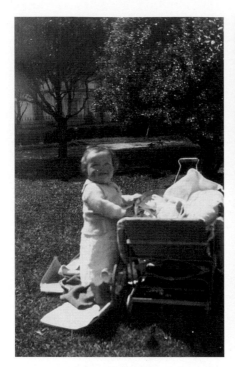

Mama was a fresh-air fanatic—all windows had to be wide open at night, and children should be outdoors as much as possible during the day. She got us out to the parks or beaches whenever it wasn't pouring rain. Maybe her attitude was a result of her experience at Cushman, where fresh air and rest were about all they had to offer the lungers.

financial problems that I was really a planned baby, but clearly once I was on the way he hoped for a boy. I was offended to learn that I had been an instant disappointment and wondered for a moment if Papa would have been any happier with a son. No, I told myself; he would have been rebellious, ungrateful, and they would have fought a lot. Then I wouldn't think about it any more.

AFTER HIS BREAKDOWN at Samuels, Papa entered a period of remarkable productivity. He turned out a rapid stream of *Black Mask* stories which, with the encouragement of editors Philip Cody and later Joseph Thompson Shaw, were longer and more fully developed. The Continental

This photo was taken on one of the Sundays when Papa would take the ferry over to visit us in Fairfax. He was always very creative about playing with us—making up games, drawing pictures on the windows with Bon Ami and making shadow puppets on the walls. He liked nicknames. Mary was the Tow Head, and I was the Little Hippo, later on Joseph Northeast (I don't remember why), and finally the Loco Princess.

This is me a couple of years after we left San Francisco. It is probably Burbank, where we lived briefly before settling in Santa Monica. The bunny is one my father sent. He usually remembered us at Easter, Christmas, and our birthdays. I remember this as a nice fuzzy bunny, but it wasn't in a class with the titanic-sized yellow ducklings he sent the following year. The other kids in the neighborhood used to look forward to our getting packages from New York.

Op, an established favorite, became more human and three-dimensional. Characters emerged who would be used more subtly in his later work: The dangerous, and often red-headed woman; the pragmatic, dogged detective; the gullible thief, who could be turned against his pals. Key themes appeared: political and personal corruption; the problem of moral ambiguity.

My favorite Op story is "Dead Yellow Women." I like it not so much for its literary interest as for its tongue-in-cheek Chinatown atmosphere. When I'm in San Francisco I can still walk up Grant to Spofford Alley and wonder which house was the one with the red-painted steps and door. I can imagine the Op whispering to the tiny slave girl and exchanging Oriental courtesies with the sinister Chang Li Ching. I admire the Op for bringing off a successful end to the case by means that were only slightly fraudulent. The story also contains one of my father's classic lines. About heroin addict Dummy Uhl, he comments: "another man whose social life had ruined him."

He was writing poetry, articles for *Western Advertising*, book reviews for *The Saturday Review of Literature*. All this while fighting off TB and trying to keep the wolf from the door—now two doors, since my parents were living apart.

His first great success came in February 1929 with the publication of *Red Harvest*. It had been serialized in *Black Mask* under the title "The Cleansing of Poisonville." The Knopf edition, with the new title, received good reviews. He had already finished *The Dain Curse*, which appeared in July of the same year. He began and completed half-a-dozen new projects during that time. He must have felt there was an endless wellspring of words inside him, that he could go on creating and writing forever.

Butte, somewhat altered, and re-christened Personville (and called "Poisonville" by those who knew it) became the central character in his first

This is an early photo of the Anaconda Copper Company smelters at Butte, Montana. It looks very much as Papa described it in *Red Harvest*, "brick stacks stuck up tall against a gloomy mountain." Papa worked for Pinkerton's here in the twenties, when the mine bosses and the Wobblies were at each other's throats. Mother grew up in Anaconda just a few miles to the west and worked in a Butte hospital during the same period Papa was there.

novel. He first saw Butte in his twenties when he was working for Pinkerton's. The agency had been brought in by the mine owners to help in their struggle with the unions and the radical IWW. Their job was to infiltrate and disrupt. What Papa did there as an undercover man, and what he saw done, left a deep and lasting impression on him.

Of all Papa's books *Red Harvest* is my favorite. I love it for its language, for its cast of unregenerate lowlifes, and most of all for its reckless energy. It seems amazing to me that as sick as Papa was, as rotten as he must have felt much of the time, he could have put that much vigor, so much explosive power, into his writing. Later he would say that it was writing that kept

Red Harvest came out in 1929, the first of Papa's novels to be published and my personal favorite. In later novels his plots got smoother and his women better coifed. But he was never funnier and his words were never truer. These are the dust jackets of the first American (top) and British editions.

him alive in those days. So, maybe it worked both ways—his energy was fed by the energy he poured into the book.

Red Harvest starts out running, gains speed as the bodies pile up, and doesn't slow down until almost everyone has met a nasty, and usually well-deserved, death. A frightening momentum builds. Even the Op, usually so cool and professional, loses his detachment and gets sucked into the carnage, goes "blood simple" as he puts it.

The Continental Op had appeared in twenty-five or more *Black Mask* stories, but this is one of the few times he is vulnerable, letting his guard down in front of a woman. Dinah Brand is rumpled, frowzy, edging into blowzy, and perfectly comfortable with herself and men—the kind of woman, I noticed over the years, that my father was attracted to. The Op is drawn to her: She can match him drink for drink and isn't snowed by his word games. "'That doesn't mean anything to me,' she tells him, 'though it sounds like it's meant to.'" She's got her priorities straight: "If a girl's got something that's worth something to somebody, she's a boob if she doesn't collect."

Dinah heads a fine cast of thugs and grifters—Pete The Finn, Whisper Thaler, Bill Quint. Dan Rolff (rhymes with cough) is a lunger, whom Dinah keeps around as a sort of house pet. His description might be Papa's: "A thin man with a tired face . . . and tired dark eyes." Papa's build and Papa's condition, but not his disposition: Rolff takes Dinah's abuse and dies a senseless death avenging her.

But most of all it's the language of *Red Harvest* I love. The characters speak in a flat American voice that finds surprise and delight in the obvious: "so you're still alive," says Dinah to the Op. "I suppose nothing can be done about it. Come on in." They've looked at the worst and not only accepted it but take comfort in it: "He's not going to die any more," says Wobbly Bill Quint over the dead body of Donald Willsson. They like Pig

Latin, euphemisms: "Grease us twice!" (for Jesus Christ) says Chief Noonan, and familiar jokes: "'Is he a criminal lawyer?' 'Yes, very.'"

He used words with precision and scorned writers who didn't. He told me once with a sneer that Mrs. Erskine Caldwell had bragged that her husband never rewrote anything. My dad said, "It shows." I remember him reciting a sentence from an Erle Stanley Gardner work—something like, "the kitchen was immaculate but a thick layer of dust lay over everything." That was the kind of sloppiness he abhorred.

Papa loved all kinds of word play: thieves' cant, convict argot, Yiddish expressions, restaurant and cowboy talk, Cockney rhyming slang, gangster-lowlife speak. Cowboyisms and Yiddish peppered his conversation. He knew that the French called their dogs "Flic" as a way of insulting the police who went by the same name. That when a waitress said a customer wants catsup, she meant he was a rube. He knew the difference between a "schlemiel" and a "schlemazzel," one a fool, and the other the victim of bad luck. What a "gunsel" really was—a boy used for immoral purposes, as Hammett said, not a gunman; and what you did on the "strawberry lay"—steal wash off backyard clothes lines. He stored away every choice bit he'd heard when he worked for the railway, when he was a kid on Baltimore streets, when he was locked up in jail doing a Pinkerton's job. What he hadn't heard himself he got out of books, and what he hadn't read, he made up. Papa had a dead-on ear for dialogue. And it's never better used than in his first full-length work.

Red Harvest comes out of *Black Mask* days. It's got *Black Mask* rough edges and give-it-all-you've-got energy. The later novels are smoother, more finely tuned. But this is the one I like best, because it's hard like its people, funny and unforgiving, and sounds most like Papa.

The same month that *The Dain Curse* was published, June 1929, he sent Knopf the manuscript of his latest novel, *The Maltese Falcon*. It was

The World March 10, 1930

This ad appeared in the *New York World* just after *The Maltese Falcon* was published. The *Falcon* got rave reviews, not only as a mystery but as a mainstream book. This must have pleased Papa mightily. I don't know if Mother realized what all this excitement was about. Of course, she was happy about having some money for a change, but I doubt she had any idea of just how big a celebrity Papa had become or what it would mean to our lives.

Papa was cat's meat for the publicists: tall, striking, distinguished, with a hazy romantic background. This advertisement for *The Glass Key* would be enough to turn anybody's head. To us it seemed to be describing someone we'd never actually met.

Papa sent Mary this postcard in May 1928 while he was in Los Angeles dickering with one of the film studios. He must have begun to feel like a celebrity himself in those heady days, though he hadn't the money yet to act like one.

published in 1930 to extraordinary reviews. He was compared to the best mainstream writers of the day.

By the fall of 1929 he was feeling prosperous for the first time in his life. Royalty checks were coming in. Warners and Fox had bought movie rights to two of the novels. San Francisco was too small for him. He'd do what writers do who have made it: He'd go to New York.

The plan was for Mother to take Mary and me down to Los Angeles. She'd like the climate better, and she wouldn't be alone. The Montana Kellys wintered there. Papa would be back and forth to see us often. He bought her a big steamer trunk and sent out for a Chinese dinner. The next morning he put us on the train for L.A.

I don't know if Mother knew about the girl Papa was going east with. If not, she must have figured it out when she saw that his next book, *The*

Glass Key, was dedicated to Nell Martin. That must have been hard on her. But no matter, I told myself later when I could understand: The dedication to *The Maltese Falcon* reads "To Jose" and that is about as good as it gets.

OUR LIFE TOGETHER was over after we left San Francisco in 1929. I never had dreams of my parents getting together again, about our living together in the same house and being a family. By then, even my mother acknowledged that family life was not for my father. When her Montana relatives made pointed remarks about her being alone, she pretended not to hear; but afterwards she told my sister and me, "they don't understand

From New York, Papa sent us snaps from his Thirty-First Street apartment window. It may have been the apartment he shared with Nell Martin, the woman he'd left San Francisco with. He had dedicated his fourth novel, *The Glass Key*, to her, but I don't think they stayed together long. Getting books dedicated to you didn't seem to be particularly lucky for Papa's ladies. He dedicated *The Maltese Falcon* to my mother, and by the time it was published, he was gone.

hence he writes very, very slowly, pondering over the keys of his machine to decide, like Oscar Wilde, whether to put in that comma or to take it out.

MR. HAMMETT'S BOOKS

Red Harvest (1929)   The Dain Curse (1929)
The Maltese Falcon (1930)   The Glass Key (1931)
The Thin Man (1934)

•

THE THIN MAN

"The best detective story yet written in America." —*Alexander Woollcott.*

"Dashiell Hammett is undoubtedly the best of American detective story writers, and 'The Thin Man' is certainly the most breathless of all his stories."—*Sinclair Lewis.*

"I think it is by far the best of Mr. Hammett's books. . . It is the usual Hammett knockout, with an additional punch."—*Herbert Asbury.*

Alfred · A · Knopf Publisher · N · Y ·

DASHIELL HAMMETT

DASHIELL HAMMETT

An ex-detective, a Pinkerton, he is today the acknowledged master of the modern American detective story. A few years ago a writer for cheap pulp magazines, today his stories are reviewed in *The New Republic,* journal of the intelligentsia. Author of only five books in a world in which writers of detective fiction are as prolific as mackerel, he has already been a Hollywood success, has appeared in the most glittering of our million-circulation magazines, and has become the favorite of Alexander Woollcott, Sinclair Lewis, Herbert Asbury, F. P. A., Jascha Heifetz and a score of equally distinguished critics and celebrities.

"There is an absolute distinction of art in his books," said *The New Republic.* "Anybody who doesn't read him misses much of modern America," said Dorothy Parker. They all say this: that his prose has the brilliance, the breathlessness, the toughness, the speed and violence of American life — that it has the impact of machine-gun fire — that there are no stories so real, so hard, so brutally exciting as his.

He is a strange and provocative personality. Undoubtedly much of the air of reality and toughness in his books, the use of the underworld vernacular of the sleuth, arise out of his own experience in the racket; yet personally he is quiet, gentle and generous. He is tall, slender, pale, with prematurely white hair and mustache. He was born in Maryland, grew up in Philadelphia, and became a detective in San Francisco. He served as a sergeant during the war and left the army with his health shattered and years of hospital before him. It was then—although he had left school at fourteen to become a newsboy, a messenger boy, a machinist, and a stevedore—that he turned to writing.

He is an indefatigable and charming host, a connoisseur of fine liquors, and an expert ping-pong player. He likes dogs and loves music. He reads endlessly — almost everything but detective stories. His favorite book is Spengler's THE DECLINE OF THE WEST and he often turns to it for bedtime reading. He likes tweeds and he owns a green suit. He smokes enormously. When in New York he may be found several nights in the week at Tony's. He writes on the typewriter and needs only one draft. He almost never rewrites anything — and

---

The Thin Man was published by Knopf in January 1934, after it had been serialized in *Redbook* the month before, and this is what the publishers sent around to publicize it. Nick and Nora Charles were to become Papa's most popular characters. But I, not quite eight, was more taken with Asta. Later on when the movie came out, Asta, now a wire-hair terrier instead of a schnauzer, was all the rage. You could buy ceramic Astas and little red fire hydrants like the Charleses had in their living room.

about Papa; how he is." He could not put up with the everyday clatter and confusion of family life. He disliked the hypocrisy of showy family holidays like Christmas. The ideal of the loving family holding hands under the Christmas tree hadn't been his experience. That attitude shows in his work, where families have rapacious mothers, wandering daughters, even fathers who kill their sons. Christmas with Nick and Nora Charles in Papa's novel *The Thin Man* was pleasant enough, but it passed in an alcoholic daze.

Papa was with us only a few Christmases in the years after 1929, when he began moving restlessly back and forth between the coasts. But during

to Jose

with wishes

for a Merry Christ-

mas from Little Jo,

Mary Jane, and Dashiell

This is the card that Papa made for my mother in the late twenties. Like everything he made, it was deceptively simple, minimal, just right.

The Beverly Wilshire
APARTMENT-HOTEL

WILSHIRE BLVD. BETWEEN El CAMINO AND RODEO DRIVES
Beverly Hills, California

From the middle thirties on the Beverly Wilshire was Papa's favorite hotel in L.A. It was a convenient place to spend money with Brock's Jewelry, Saks, and Viennese Chocolates within walking distance and the Brown Derby just across the street. On December 26, 1937 Papa sent a letter to Lillian on hotel stationery, marking the windows of his penthouse suite, which was said to have six bedrooms.

our times together he made every day seem like Christmas. We caught glimpses of a different world when we visited him at his hotels or at his rented houses in Bel Air and Malibu. The light had a golden feel; there was more space; things smelled different. Everything he had was in such wonderful taste—the gold pen, the silver cigarette cases, a white cable-knit sweater.

He was proud of my sister and me. We got to stay overnight at his hotels in Hollywood—the Ambassador, the Roosevelt, and later the Beverly Wilshire. He took Mary to the fights at the old Olympic Gardens and me (five years younger) to the races at Santa Anita. There were lunches at the Brown Derby and dinners at Chasen's. He gave us extravagant presents at whim—gold-link bracelets that spelled out our names, elaborate boxes of European chocolates for Mother. He loved giving gifts, and

Me and Mary with the Raggedy Andy doll Papa sent from FAO Schwartz in New York. There was a Raggedy Ann that went with it. He loved buying us things. The more extravagant gifts came for no reason at all. I look to be about four in this picture, which was my age when I first met Lillian.

we loved getting them. He gave us child-sized Raggedy Ann and Andys, stuffed Easter ducks larger than geese. One day a trunk-sized box of toys from FAO Schwartz arrived. It included a Punch and Judy stage and a dozen puppets, games, dolls, and puzzles—a child's fantasy. Looking back I can see that the gifts were probably an attempt to make up for being absent so much of the time—I knew it even then. And, of course, in retrospect I can see it would have been smarter for him to have started college funds for us or maybe to have set up an annuity. But that would have been someone else's father, not ours, who had never dreamed of living much past thirty or of being famous or of having money to burn.

Tuberculosis marked and stiffened him. His illness caused him to conclude that it was useless to take good care of yourself. He told me that the guys in the army hospital who followed the doctor's orders, got lots of rest and good nights' sleep, did worse than those like himself who sneaked out to town and smoked, drank, and helled around when they could. He believed that the disease respected toughness, a quality that my father admired greatly. "I can stand anything I've got to stand," Ned Beaumont says in *The Glass Key*. That could have been Papa's motto.

Mama in the 30s. She was courageous, tough, and, most of the time, cheerful.

STANDING TOUGH

"Will I suffer—much?"

"A couple of bad days; but they won't be as bad as you'll think they are, and your father's toughness will carry you through them."

EXCHANGE BETWEEN GABRIELLE LEGGETT AND THE OP,
THE DAIN CURSE, CHAPTER TWENTY

In those days before men were supposed to be sensitive it was okay to be tough. My father admired tough men and tough women—people like Babe Ruth, who was still making it around the bases in the last stages of syphilis; guys like Ned Beaumont in The Glass Key *who says, "I can stand anything I've got to stand"; women like my mother who put off going to the hospital to have her babies till the last moment.*

Papa liked tough sports. Boxing was a favorite. Joe Louis's visit to the Aleutians was one of the rare times he seemed impressed by a celebrity. When he was in L.A. he went to the old Olympic Gardens arena. He took my mother once and, strangely enough, she appeared to enjoy it, though she was shocked that one of the Latino boxers was called "Jesus" and crossed himself before the bout began.

Papa was a Yankee fan in baseball season and liked the Chicago Bears in football. He thought the college stuff, with its pom-pom high jinks, was silly. He teased me about my team, the

UCLA Bruins, bringing the band out at half time to form a pink carnation.

He was proud of his Pinkerton's days when toughness counted. One of my earliest memories is of getting to feel the dent in his head from being hit by a brick when he bungled a tailing job, and he let me see the knife tip embedded in the palm of his hand. He would tighten up his stomach muscles and tell my sister and me "Hit me as hard as you can. Harder!" And we would hit him hard, as hard as little girls could. He showed us how to break a hand hold by pinching back the little finger. I tried it once on the playground with disastrous results.

Toughness was the quality that would take him through the last bad years—prison, sickness, money problems, Mary. In a world where roof beams were always in danger of falling, toughness is all you could count on.

Once when I was eight or nine, and Papa was singing my praises to Lillian, he concluded with, "And she's tough." The incident stayed in my memory as the first time it ever occurred to me that Papa might not be one hundred percent correct in his judgments, all of the time. And the sentence had an ominous ring to it—like maybe I would have to be.

...

Once when I was eight or nine Papa talked to Mary and me about fear. We were in the living room of the house on Ninth Street in Santa Monica; Mama was out in the kitchen. I don't remember what brought it on—something Mary or I had done, I guess. But what he said was that it was crazy to worry about everything that might happen. "Hey," he said looking up at the ceiling, "The roof might fall in; anything could happen. But you can't go around worrying about that kind of stuff." He paused and added, "Your mother is afraid of everything." It was as if to say that he knew why Mama was like that and even sympathized; he just didn't want it to rub off on us.

He was right about Mama. She was afraid most of the time. And with darned good reason, I thought. She'd had a childhood right out of Dickens, and nothing much had gone well after that. The thing about Mama, though, was that while she was afraid of almost everything—landlords, driving, water heaters, priests, escalators, toasters and telephones—she went right on dealing with them. She never chickened out.

Both my parents were brave that way—maybe Mother more so than Papa, because she was more fearful. But Papa had his phobias too. He just didn't advertise them. He disliked flying. Once just before he was due to fly east he was changing a light bulb for my mother when it exploded in his hand. "That's probably what the plane will do," he said to her. Later, when I had an appointment with my doctor, he asked me to get him a couple of sleeping pills for the flight.

He was claustrophobic too, which must have been hard later when he went to prison. I had a strange sort of déjà vu experience at the San Francisco Post Street apartment building where he wrote *The Maltese Falcon* in 1929. We had been up visiting his fourth-floor apartment, now occupied by my friend Bill Arney, and five of us crowded into the elevator for the ride to the lobby. The elevator, with its folding brass grille, is the original in the 1917 building, and, I later learned, the last one with rope cable in the city. We squeezed ourselves into its tiny cage, and as we started down I shut my eyes and tried to empty my mind. But a sudden impression came rushing in—of how Papa, seventy years earlier, would have felt trapped in here—stomach constricted, air pulled out of his lungs, the walls pushing in, the light starting to fade. I shook off the vision and told myself that was nonsense. He would have taken the stairs. No, I corrected myself; he was too sick then. He would have needed to save every drop of energy. Besides he wouldn't have given in to being afraid. Okay, I conceded, but *damn* he must have hated getting into that little box.

In southern California we moved around at first, from a bungalow court in Hollywood to a house in Beverly Hills. We got a live-in maid, a big Swedish woman, but she didn't last. We were naughty children with Papa not around. We stuck out our tongues and drew crayon scribbles on her door. The maid left and was not replaced. Mother was not used to servants, and she was not comfortable in Beverly Hills. When she took us to the park there were few children, and those were with maids.

We moved to West L.A., Burbank, Glendale. Papa bought Mama a brand-new Packard but didn't keep up the payments. A process server came, and when Mama wouldn't take the paper, he threw it in the driveway. The next day the Packard was gone, and after that we had to take the bus or the Red Line. But Mama didn't mind about that. She hated driving and had to lie down afterwards with a damp towel over her eyes.

In the middle thirties we settled in Santa Monica, a pretty beach town. We could walk to St. Monica's Church and to the beach in the summer.

Everybody liked Mother, felt easy with her. Strange ladies sat down next to her at the bus stop and poured out their troubles. Mrs. Donagan from across the street brought over a bottle of port wine, and they sat in the kitchen while she complained about an out-of-work husband and an ungrateful daughter. Mother sipped the port and listened sympathetically, but she secretly disapproved. It was not her way, this running around the neighborhood airing your dirty linen. You kept your problems to yourself, or at least in the family—if you had one, which we didn't. We were all alone in southern California.

Mother made acquaintances easily, but she did not cultivate close friends. I have sometimes wondered if it would have made a difference if she had had a friend who could ask the occasional question, "So, Jose, do you think Mr. Hammett will ever come back and live with you and the girls again?" Or, "Have you ever thought of going back to nursing? Maybe meet someone, get married again?" What would she have answered? I can't imagine, because I can't imagine her having such a conversation.

Mother was tough; she would fight like a tiger if one of us were threatened. But along with this was a terrible passivity that let her endure long years alone, till age put out the final spark of hope. For me her story is more tragic than my father's. He chose his isolation, but mother just let it happen by default. She could have had a life, found a new husband, and had some companionship and security. Maybe. Maybe not. I realize that I didn't know her any more than my children know me. Perhaps staying faithful to my father was the only thing she could have done. Maybe she had no choice at all.

His attitude toward her was as to a cherished younger sister whom he admired for her grit. He said she would hold up fine if you came in with your head half hacked off, but went to pieces if you got an itty-bitty cut on your finger. He'd had a terrible time getting her to go to the hospital with us girls.

As a nurse she'd seen too many new mothers hanging around for hours before their babies came, so she insisted on waiting till the last moment.

IN THE EARLY thirties Mother made an appointment to have her picture taken, a studio portrait. She cut her hair, saving the braid in a black cotton stocking, which I later found among her boxes. She bought a dress with a lace collar and put on make-up. The photographer took six different poses. In most of them she was smiling, but in the one she chose to send to my father she is not. She sits rigid, staring straight ahead, eyes intent under unplucked eyebrows. The make-up is all wrong. The lipstick gives her mouth an unnatural shape. She hardly used it, didn't know how. Her hair, still thick but shorter, was marcelled into rigid plastic waves. She thought about enclosing a note, but decided against it, and mailed the portrait off to New York.

This is the portrait that Mother had taken in the mid-thirties to send to Papa in New York. She had just recently had her hair cut short and began to have it marcelled. That style was all the rage, but I never thought it suited her. Mother had beautiful chestnut-brown hair, and, when we were small, she would turn out the lights so we could see the sparks when she brushed it.

I imagine my father receiving it. He has let the mail pile up and opens it all Sunday afternoon, very hung-over. He sees the portrait, sees what it is. He puts it back in its envelope and shoves it in a drawer, where it will stay until he moves, and it is discarded along with other odds and ends. Papa was not a saver of things.

LILLIAN WAS THE BOOGIE MAN of my childhood. Her name in my mother's mouth had a cold, scary sound. And it was always "Lillian"—not "Lillian Hellman" or "Miss Hellman" as it might have been in those more formal times—but "Lillian," as if she knew her, as if they had met, which of course they had not and never would.

The gossip columns were full of my dad and Lillian. The Montana

CHUTZPA

Papa admired people who went too far, who did the crazily audacious. Like the great uncle who rubbed pepper in his eyes to punish himself for oversleeping, the comic who told jokes about the Titanic *sinking. Like Lillian.*

He admired people who didn't count the cost, who went beyond what was reasonable. You made your choice, gave it your best shot. And if you were wrong you paid for it. No whining, no excuses. In The Glass Key *when Ned Beaumont tells Senator Henry, "You'll take what's coming to you"—denying him the "easy way" out—there's no doubt he was talking for my father.*

relatives sent clippings and their indignation. Mother was humiliated and terrified that they might marry. Her public stance was that although she and my father might be living apart (temporarily), it was only because of Papa's need for solitude and space for his writing.

It's hard to remember how disgraceful divorce was at that time, especially for a Catholic. "Grass widow" was all you needed to say about a

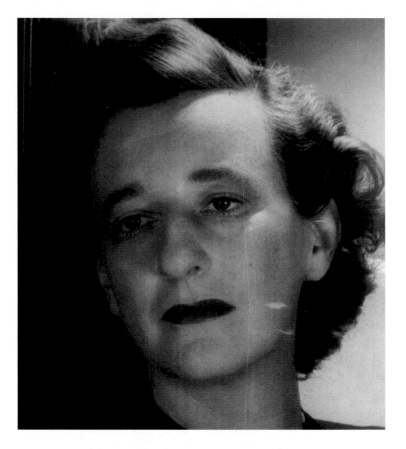

This photo of Lillian was the only one of her in my mother's album. Mama's attitude toward her changed over the years from kind of a horrified dread in the early days and later to acceptance, and even appreciation, for the care she had given to Papa when he most needed it. My own attitude toward Lillian has veered wildly between admiration and righteous indignation—the latter being the one most often urged on me by others. But every time I thought of the manipulative, mendacious, bad-tempered Lillian, I remembered the funny, generous, high-spirited one. The only solution, so far, has been to think of Lillian in the same way I think of cholesterol. There is good cholesterol and bad cholesterol. They often work at odds, but they're there in the same system, use the same name, and can't be separated out. It's a schizo, inadequate accommodation, but the best I have come up with.

Lillian in her twenties. She was only a little older when I first met her. I much admired her taste in clothes. She was always perfectly dressed for the occasion. Her style was more continental and elegant than I would have chosen for myself, but it suited her. Lillian was especially proud of her diminutive feet (which contrasted badly with Mary's and my number-eights) and kept a large array of shoes on hand. She had a wall of shoe storage built into one home in Beverly Hills, which I considered the last word in sophisticated living.

Though he would never have said so, Papa was deeply disappointed in himself. He wanted to be regarded as a serious author, like the pals he drank with—the Faulkners and Fitzgeralds. But he never thought he quite brought it off. Yet he knew he was good at what he did—maybe the best. Certainly he was one of the most imitated. "I've been as bad an influence on American literature as anyone I can think of," he said. A typed copy of Raymond Chandler's "The Simple Art of Murder," a sincere and eloquent tribute to his work, was one of the few personal items he saved. He was proud of his work, but he wanted to do more.

woman, and you knew what she was. Mother was in her own way proud. I only remember her asking me to lie one time, when I was four. Papa had gone back to New York, and the Montana relatives were visiting. Mary wakened me from my nap and gave me my instructions: "We've been to New York, and you didn't think the buildings were so tall." Even at four, well before I could have put it into words, I understood. Mother had said we had been with Papa in New York, and I mustn't let her down. In the living room before the gathered relatives I performed faithfully. Everyone laughed, and I saw Mother relax. She needn't have worried. With us nothing had to be explained.

I never fully realized, however, the force of her desperation until years later when she told me she had actually gone to see Arthur Kober, Lillian's then husband, and asked if he and Lillian were divorcing. Kober, kindly, and, I imagine, greatly embarrassed, said no, no divorce was planned. The affair was just one of those Hollywood flings and would soon pass, he said. Mother took what comfort she could from that.

In later times the only negative thing I remember my mother saying about Lillian was that she thought Lillian should have given Mary and me some of my dad's things after his death.

THE AMAZING NEW HOOVER

My father was a great storyteller, but Lillian was even better. On one of her last trips to the West Coast she was remembering the early days in New York. It was in the thirties. She had an apartment she liked in a good location with a rent she could afford. She did something that miffed my dad—what I don't know. He decided to take revenge.

In those days the paper always ran a coupon saying something like, "Get your carpet vacuumed free. See the amazing new Hoover." He began clipping coupons and filling them out with her name and address. He gathered coupons from every paper and magazine he could find, clipped, and mailed. Then he hired a secretary to help him. The solicitations began arriving at her apartment by the dozens, followed by phone calls and salesmen. It was deep in the Depression, and men were desperate for a sale. Finally the crunch of mail and salesmen got so annoying the manager asked her to move. Papa had his revenge. Lillian told this story with about equal parts of admiration and irritation.

IN THE SUMMER of 1937 I took horseback riding lessons at the YWCA. We met once a week at the Santa Monica Y and drove down to a stable near what is now LAX. When Papa heard about this he immediately said I must have riding clothes, so one Saturday he sent a Tanner Limo for me, and we went shopping at the English Riding Shop in the Beverly Wilshire Hotel,

This is me at about ten in the riding outfit Papa bought me in the shop at the Beverly Wilshire. The stables where my group from the Santa Monica Y rode were where LAX now stands. They were rather ramshackle and set among bean fields. I was somewhat overdressed, as the other kids all rode western and wore jeans and cowboy boots.

where he was staying. The clerk asked me what style I rode. I told him English, proudly. All the other kids rode western, but I insisted on English. The little saddle was scary at first, there was no big horn to hang on to, but I loved the way it looked in pictures and in the movies. Classy. Aristocratic. The clerk brought out jodhpurs and jackets.

Lillian arrived. She spoke nicely to me, but when the clerk offered her a chair she snapped at him rudely that she didn't want to sit down. I was embarrassed, but when I glanced over at Papa he looked indulgent, as if she were a cute little kid acting up. If I had said that he would have come down on me like a ton of bricks. I had already figured out that adults could get away with about anything they want.

I went into the dressing room to try on the jodhpurs. We settled on them, boots, and a jacket. The clerk asked me solicitously if I wouldn't like a windbreaker, too. I said no thank you, not being sure what one was. "Conservative," the clerk said, complimenting Papa on my thrift. Lillian was smoking and looking bored. I thought, "'Conservative' is not a word she thinks much of."

I rode with the Y group all that summer and most of the next—until I was thrown by a big gelding called Strawberry and then fell off another horse cantering back to the stable. I got right back on like you're supposed to, but after that riding wasn't much fun.

IN THE THIRTIES my father's favorite game was Chemin de Fer. He came to the house for dinner one night and, over Mama's lemon meringue pie, gave us all new fifty-dollar bills. That was big money for an eight-year-old in the days when I could go to the matinee at the Criterion for a dime and get a hamburger in Ocean Park for a nickel. He'd won big at the Clover Club—a favorite hangout at Sunset Boulevard and La Cienega in Los Angeles. He liked Chemin de Fer I think because it was the kind of go-for-broke, all-on-the-turn-of-a-card, in-your-face game that appealed to him. Papa was reckless, prodigal. Spend it if you've got it; forget about the balance in the checkbook—if you bother to keep one at all. Burn that candle at both ends, as Edna St. Vincent Millay, a poet he particularly detested, had it.

The first time I realized this quality in him was the afternoon he took me to the races at Santa Anita. I was maybe nine or ten. I'd been permitted to take the day off from school, and we'd had a lovely day. Papa had lost a pile on a horse named Top Row, if I remember right. Over lunch in the clubhouse we bumped into Slapsy Maxie Rosenbloom, a onetime boxer then doing comic bits in the movies. He was the kind of character Nick Charles was always running into. Slapsy looked sheepish and told my dad how much he'd lost. "Yeah, sure," said my dad when he left. "He owes me money." I got the feeling that a lot of people owed him money.

Going home in the limo I was chattering away, and he was silent. When I looked over at him, I realized with a jolt that he was worried. It came to me in a flash that he had bet—and, that day—lost too much.

I knew that he had lost a lot, but the idea that he had actually bet more than he could afford to lose was almost outside my comprehension. Nobody I knew did such things. Mother worried over every dollar. It was during the depths of the Depression, and our neighbors counted their blessings if they had any kind of a steady job. Only two families on the block owned a car. I had just assumed that Papa had all the money he needed. The truth was that until the fifties we had no idea at all of his financial status.

But even at nine I knew you didn't spend what you don't have, especially on something as frivolous as horse racing. I knew about budgets, although our income was never steady enough for Mama to keep one. I was shocked and disapproving of Papa's behavior—or the ant part of me was anyway. Another part, the grasshopper, was lost in admiration. It seemed to me the most marvelous kind of bravery to plunge ahead into the unknown, disregarding all possible consequences. To risk everything on a chance: it was something I could never do, but, oh, I envied those who did. That was Papa. Papa was reckless.

This publicity portrait of Papa from the thirties makes him look pretty darn romantic. It is strange how Papa's identity got all mixed up with that of Nick Charles and the Thin Man. The title really refers to Clyde Wynant, the murder victim, of course. I suppose Papa's vague resemblance to actor William Powell compounded matters. Will the real Thin Man please stand up?

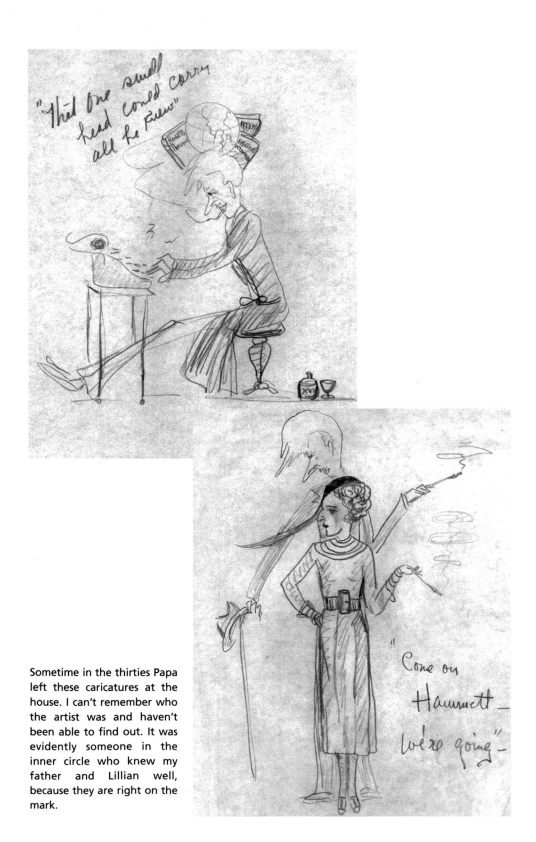

Sometime in the thirties Papa left these caricatures at the house. I can't remember who the artist was and haven't been able to find out. It was evidently someone in the inner circle who knew my father and Lillian well, because they are right on the mark.

BIASES

My dad had never cared for Leonard Bernstein. Said he was a "homo-exhibitionist" and that he didn't mind the homo but hated the exhibitionist part. Actually I think he probably did mind the homo part, at least a bit. He was very tolerant for those days, but he had his biases. He told my sister that of course there were lots of "them" in the arts, but he hadn't found them really creative, just arty. But he was sympathetic to any eccentricity if the person was honest about it. He liked to tell the story about the director who said to Charles Laughton (an open homosexual), "For Christ's sake, Charley, not so swishy!" Laughton sighed apologetically: "Sorry, it just comes out when I'm tired."

He had begun life with the usual racial biases too. His Maryland ancestors had been slave owners, and his early stories are full of the normal stereotypes—comic Negroes, sinister Orientals, and the rest. The prevalent attitude when I was small was that, "Yes, you ought to treat minorities fairly, but only if they stayed in their place." Papa had begun by accepting this attitude, but he grew out of it.

In the early forties he belonged to an organization called something like "Negroes and Allies" and showed me his membership card with pride. He laughed at his friends who said, "Well, sure there are some fine Colored, like Paul Robeson and Jackie Robinson." He pointed out to me that this was admitting that your superiors are your equals. And he noted that in the nightclubs and cafés where Negroes played or sang they could not be seated in the audience.

···

Papa enjoyed musical comedies, though he often found unintended humor in them, like the line of obviously gay chorus boys singing "There's Nothing Like a Dame" in *South Pacific*. He said the hit number from the same show, "Some Enchanted Evening," reminded him of the all the parties when he'd seen some enchanting face on the other side of the room who proved, at a closer look, not to be. The Ezio Pinza role in the Broadway production, he wrote me rather wistfully, had given men of his age group (he was 55 then) hope that they might still be a hit with the ladies.

One afternoon in 1937 Papa came in whistling "Foggy Day in London Town." At RKO Studios they were filming *Damsel in Distress*, starring Fred Astaire, and he had seen the rushes. It was a Gershwin tune: music by George, lyric by Ira. Papa really liked Ira Gershwin and his inventive, offhand way with rhyme. He would sing, "I'm bidin' my time/Cause that's the kinda guy I'm."

Papa wasn't a close friend of George Gershwin's, but they hung out with the same Hollywood crowd. Papa respected his work but found him sometimes hard to take personally. He was grandly egotistical and often condescending, particularly toward Ira, who went out of his way to keep in the background. At one time Ira even used an alias so as not to trade on his brother's fame. George also had an envious streak. Papa told a story about him sitting in a Paris café with a friend, just after he first heard Ravel's immensely popular "Bolero." He kept pounding his fist on the table and saying. "It's just a trick! It's just a trick! But it's a good trick!"

Gershwin was considered a hypochondriac by his friends. It was discovered after his death that many of the symptoms he had complained about—which even his analyst had written off as neurotic—were early

Here I am after being confirmed at Saint Monica's. Papa's attitude toward religion was unambiguous. He scoffed at it, which was the conventional stance for intellectuals of his time and place. However once I remember him saying that if he had to choose he'd be a Buddhist, because all they were supposed to do was live a good life. I don't think he went into that very deeply. Religion just had no appeal for him. I looked upon it as if he were color-blind or tone-deaf.

warnings of the brain tumor. His death in July 1937 came as a tremendous shock. Papa came by the house after the funeral, grim-faced and silent. Gershwin was only thirty-nine when he died —four years younger than my father—and they'd had much in common: Both were displaced Easterners, boys from poor families who had made it on their own. And what Gershwin had accomplished in his field—bridging the gap from Tin Pan Alley to the concert hall—was precisely parallel to what Papa wanted to do in his own.

PAPA WOULD COME and stay with us sometimes in the thirties—when he was drinking and things were not going well with him. Our house was a refuge from his other worlds. My mother cooked and tended to him, tried to get him to eat. After dinner when Mary and Mother were out in the kitchen doing dishes, Papa and I would sit together on the living room couch looking at magazines. Papa got us subscriptions sometimes when he got his own. We took *New Masses*, mostly for Mary, but I read some of the articles—about the war in Spain or poor people working in factories—and studied the black-and-white sketches of lynchings and strike breakers. We took *Fortune,* a different kind of magazine then, too, which I guess Papa read on the principle that you should know your enemy. I admired the bold, futuristic designs on the covers and the colorful graphs inside, though I didn't read the articles. But the magazine I liked best was *The New Yorker.* I read the movie and play reviews, "The Talk of the Town," and the "Letter from Paris." It was the magazine Papa usually picked up to look through when he came over for dinner.

Papa studied each page carefully—the advertisements, the verse, the funny bits at the bottom on fractured English or incoherent ads. He sent in one of those items himself he told me, and they sent him five dollars for it. The cartoons got special attention. He liked William Steig, with his tough little kids, Whitney Darrow, and Charles Addams's weird family. He pointed out Uncle Imar peering out of the attic window. Papa lingered over every page, seeing things I would have skipped over. He had an intense interest in the details of life. Almost nothing escaped his notice.

The New Yorker for me was a window on Papa's life away from us. When I looked at it with him I felt I was a part of its smart sophisticated scene that included blasé show girls and lecherous businessmen, gold diggers and mink-coated matrons. I was an insider who could get the same jokes, enjoy the same books, pan the same movies. If given the chance, I could be just as witty as Dotty Parker and as urbane as Peter Arno. The feeling didn't last, I knew, but for those minutes sitting next to Papa on the couch, I felt perfectly at home in his shiny *New Yorker* world.

SO MANY BOOKS

Papa was an omnivorous reader. He wrote my mother in June of 1927 that he had bought a set of encyclopedias. He probably devoured it cover to cover.

That was apparently the source of many of his plot ideas. "Lock me in a room with a set of encyclopedias, and I'll come up with a plot," he used to say. His idea of heaven was going cross-country in a train compartment, in his pajamas, reading all the way. He read The Critique of Pure Reason *at thirteen (looking for absolute truth). Not burdened with any academic baggage, he made his own judgments: he loved Dostoyevski, thought him funny; he thought Dickens had wonderful characters but didn't know what to do with them. He said of Robert Graves's* Hercules My Shipmate, *"That the way a novel's supposed to be." He said*

Hemingway couldn't write love scenes. When Death of a Salesman *got raves, he said he hadn't seen it, but he doubted Arthur Miller was capable of anything that good.*

*He read the tonier magazines—*The New Yorker, Atlantic, Fortune—*but he also liked trade mags that told you what was new in cement mixing and Jersey breeding. He took the leftist* New Masses *and read* Time, *though he sneered at it, and kidded me about reading* Life, *the other Luce rag.*

He liked sci-fi—Doc Savage—and the comics—Terry and the Pirates and Snuffy Smith (a real hillbilly unlike the phony Li'l Abner). He admired Don Marquis, the inspired author of Archy and Mehitabel—*the gusty little cockraoch who couldn't work the capitals and the trampy lady cat, down but never out.*

1937. I WAS ten and Mary, fifteen. We were living in the stucco house on Ninth Street in Santa Monica, with the big toyon over the front porch. Mother had taken the Red Line to downtown L.A. and had just come back with two May Co. dresses for me, and vegetables from the Grand Central Market. We were all in the living room, when Papa arrived unexpectedly. He kissed us, as usual, but acted nervous and uneasy. He said something low to Mama, and she told us to go put away the vegetables. We went out to the kitchen, surprised. This had never happened before.

The kitchen door was the swinging kind with gaps at the top and bottom, and there was only the dining room between us and the living room. Mary went over to the vegetables on the counter and rattled the paper bags

Papa and Mary at Malibu. Mary was only thirteen in this picture, but she always looked older. Papa liked to take her out to dinner at nice places and to boxing matches. I was only a little jealous, because he took me to lunch at the Brown Derby and let me stay out of school to go to the races at Santa Anita.

as if we were unwrapping the celery. Then we both crowded up against the door and tried to hear what was being said.

Mary edged me out of the best position, and I could only hear a murmur of voices. But she could hear snatches of what was going on—or at least she pretended she could. She gave me several versions of what was being said, then settled on one: "They're getting a divorce, and he wants you! Well, he's not going to get you!" she added heroically.

It was at this moment that I lost all faith in Mary as interpreter. The idea of Papa wanting to take me away from Mother was ridiculous. I know my father loved me but not any more than he loved Mary. And he'd never have done anything that mean to Mama. Besides, he'd have asked me, and I'd have told him no, that it was fun sleeping over at the Beverly Wilshire or one of the big houses he rented, but not forever. I'd have missed Mama and the cats too much. The fact that he might have been asking for a

This is the house in Santa Monica where we lived the longest. Papa would come over to dinner, and sometimes when he was drinking he'd stay overnight. Our landlady was rather eccentric and didn't believe in trimming anything, so the toyon obscured the front of the house, and the backyard was like a jungle. The cats and I loved it.

divorce was not particularly disturbing. He didn't live with us anyhow, so what difference would it make? He would still be our father. I knew Catholics aren't supposed to get divorces, but sometimes they did anyway. If you don't get married again, and I couldn't have imagined Mama doing that, it didn't seem to matter.

They talked a long while, Papa's voice going up and down and Mama's just a murmur. And then we heard them at the dining-room table and the rustle of papers. The front door closed. Papa was gone, and we came out of the kitchen. Mother's eyes were shiny, and she was blowing her nose. She said nothing to us and started dinner.

Mary was right—about the divorce anyway. We heard Mother talking to one of her relatives, who was a lawyer. It was one of those Mexican mail-order jobs, he told her, and was probably invalid. Mama took what consolation she could from that.

I was puzzled about how sad and, somehow, ashamed the divorce—legal or not—made her. What had meant little to me—about how we lived or thought of each other—seemed to mean a great deal to her.

ONE BEAUTIFUL SUMMER day in the forties, my father and I were out on the lawn in the backyard of my mother's house in West L.A. There was a blanket on the grass and cards spread out. My father had been playing solitaire. He was in a good mood, leaning back against the lawn chair, wearing trunks and the sandals he'd asked me to find in Westwood. And out of nowhere particular he told me the Flitcraft story.

I admit that I hadn't read *The Maltese Falcon* since I was in grade school, and the story seemed unconnected. But he told it as a story he had just heard or read, not as if he had used it as a set-piece in a book. He told it with such delight and enjoyment, like a funny story you want to share

PAPA'S JOKES

After more than forty years Papa still makes me laugh—his sticker on an envelope from the '40s "Bibles for Russians" and the cut-out signature of Erle Stanley Gardner on the bottom of a letter. It is what I remember most about him—how funny he was and how much fun he was to be with. He was a great storyteller. He told us about being at some political meeting where the chair was calling for someone with great courage and selflessness to undertake a particularly dangerous job. "Hell, what we need here is an intelligent coward," he responded.

Many of his stories seemed pretty racy in those days: Joan Crawford to King Vidor on her way to take a shower before having sex with him, "Start without me if you want."

He found the humor implicit in everyday life. The diaper service that advertized, "We're tops for your baby's bottom." He liked weird names—a local sports writer's byline, "Syd Zyff," caught his fancy. During the notorious Overell-Gollum trial in L.A. he noted that the jurors were equally divided among the sexes and explained that that was so they would each have a roommate if they had to be sequestered. He had a clear eye for what was ridiculous, banal, sham.

This is the backyard of the house on Purdue that Papa bought Mama. In the forties he would come and stay with us, barbecue chicken on the grill, and putter around the house doing odd jobs for Mother. He loved to lie out on the back lawn and play solitaire. Insects never bothered him, he said; they were put off by the taste of tobacco and booze. When I was at UCLA he would sometimes help me with assignments. Once he lettered in some information on a map. It turned out much neater than I could ever have done. We'd talk about my classes; usually he knew much more about the subject matter than I did.

while it's still fresh in your mind. It was both old to him and new. He told it as if it was sweet to him, a thing he had savored and relished that he wanted me to share.

Papa plunged into the story without any explanation. The words he used were identical with those Sam Spade uses. In Tacoma one midday a local businessman left his office to go out to lunch. On his way to the restaurant, passing an office building under construction, a beam came crashing down to the street barely missing him. He wasn't really hurt except for a scrape on his cheek, but he was badly shaken, more shocked than scared. He felt as if someone had taken the lid off life and let him look inside.

He had been leading a nice, orderly, reasonable life, with a wife, two sons, and a successful business. He'd been content because he'd believed that the world was a nice, orderly, reasonable place. Now he saw that that was an illusion. The world was chaotic. People lived and died by pure chance. It was a random universe, and by living in an orderly way, he had gotten out of sync with it. He left the city that day, left his business, his wife and children, and never went back. It seemed to him that by acting in a random way he could get back in step with the universe.

Years later he was found living in Spokane, with a business, two children, and a wife, who was more like his first than not. He wasn't sorry for what he'd done. It didn't seem strange to him that he had gone back to living the same kind of orderly life he'd led in Tacoma. And this was the part Papa liked best: That he'd gotten used to beams falling, then when they didn't fall, he got used to that, too.

What I remember is his delight in the story—as if it were a gift he had received that was just right. As a boy he had wanted to find the Ultimate Truth—how the world operated. And here it was. There was no system except blind chance. Beams falling.

IN JULY 1941 my sister and I took the train from Union Station in L.A. to New York to spend the summer with Papa. I was a young fifteen and Mary a sophisticated nineteen. It was our first trip east, and we were very excited.

In Chicago, pulling into the rail yards we got a startling glimpse of eastern-style poverty. The tracks there ran parallel to a tall row of weathered wooden tenements, their balconies hung with flapping laundry. Young black men in their undershirts, leaning on the balcony railings,

This photo of Papa dates from 1939. He had stopped working for MGM and was working on a new novel that was never finished. He was living at the Plaza hotel in New York and was busy helping start *PM*, the short-lived leftist newspaper.

seemed to be looking directly into our dining car. I knew about poverty. I'd seen the poorer parts of Santa Monica. In the thirties if you walked south of Broadway you passed abruptly from our pleasant small-town America to another world of unpaved streets, dusty fields, women cooking over open fires in the yards of tumble-down shacks. But there was plenty of space and an occasional geranium or oleander to give it color. It had merely looked picturesque to me. And I'd read James T. Farrell's *Studs Lonigan Trilogy*, which was set in Chicago, but I had imagined nothing like this concentration of misery in buildings that must have been drafty and bitterly cold in winter and unbearably hot in summer. I thought, this is the part of America Papa had seen at first hand. It's what he wants to change.

This picture was taken in 1941 when Mary and I visited Papa in New York. I remember that outfit. I had bought it at Lord & Taylor that morning, when Papa gave us money and we hit the stores. I guess I should have been wowed at being in the Stork Club and the other glitzy spots in the city, but I disliked places where there was much drinking going on. (I don't remember what's in my glass. Probably ginger ale.) I was much happier when we were up at Hardscrabble Farm. Papa was too.

PRIVATE PAPA

Lillian once, on the subject of psychiatrists (perhaps in regard to my sister) said that my father was one of those people who thought that they could see right through you; nothing could be hidden from them. This surprised me because from my observation both of them were terribly gullible. I knew that in my sister's case the psychiatrists seemed to believe any nonsense she fed them. Her account of how she started drinking, my father told me, was that my mother always served wine with dinner, which was ridiculous.

Lillian's observation may have been true, however. When Papa was sober he kept himself to himself. He was in control, impenetrable, private. When I think back to all the things I might have asked him—about his family, his early days, the stories and novels—I kick myself that I didn't. But he just was not someone you put questions to. What he offered you took, but you didn't ask for more.

The kindest thing Lillian ever said to me came one day after she told me how much he loved me, and my response was that I couldn't really talk to him. She said, "It didn't matter. It didn't matter at all." She was right in that, I think. It didn't.

It's what he cares so much about. I wondered too what the young black men were feeling while they were looking into our dining car at us eating a pleasant lunch, waited on by black men in white coats. It was a scary thought, and I didn't linger over it.

We'd come totally unprepared for the New York heat. Mother had taken us to Bullocks and bought us matching wool suits, mine in cranberry, Mary's in teal blue. I don't know what she was thinking. We wore them on the train and then never again. The first week Papa gave us money, and we went to Lord & Taylor and bought new summer outfits. He loved buying things for us.

In the city we stayed at his hotel near Washington Square. He had a roomy two-bedroom apartment. We ordered our meals from room service, which was fine, except for my morning cocoa, bitter imported stuff made with water. Papa sent it back asking for milk, but what I got was no better. I missed Mama's sweet, milky Baker's and switched to tea.

Papa loved New York and showed it off as if it belonged to him. He took us up in the Empire State Building, we went to Jones Beach, a Dodgers game. He liked the Dodgers but disliked the Dodgers fans for the way they could turn on their team when they were losing. We saw *Hellzapoppin'* and *Pal Joey*. He bragged to Lillian that we laughed our heads off at the off-color jokes. No priggish daughters wanted here.

We went to see the movie premiere of *The Little Foxes* (with Bette Davis as Regina). He thought she was adequate but was irked that she got the final shot (it was in her contract, he said) when the young lovers should have had it. He said Tallulah Bankhead (Regina on Broadway) was ruined as an actress once she fell in love with the sound of her own voice.

The theater was the occasion of the first instance when I remember being aware that my father might not be altogether truthful all the time. He took Mary and me backstage to meet Ethyl Barrymore who was

Papa asked me to get a portrait shot taken, and this is the one I sent. He said I looked very Irish. I presumed that was a good thing.

starring in *The Corn Is Green*. She was charming to us and very regal. In a parting remark she said something to him about the play having "great social significance," perhaps thinking that would strike a sympathetic cord with him. He was quick to agree, "Oh, yes, absolutely." I could tell by the look on his face he was thinking, "Yeah, about as much as Krazy Kat."

We went to see Ethel Merman in *Panama Hattie*, even though he disliked Merman as a performer. When there was a supposedly ad-lib moment in which she playfully tickled the little girl in the cast, the child flinched and Papa whispered, "Looks like she's been slapping the kid again." I didn't take this to mean that he really knew that Merman had been doing that, but that it was the kind of thing that she might do.

Papa had a generally low opinion of actors. He despised their self-preoccupation and their ruthlessness. He and Lillian once toyed with a young actress by shifting the conversation every which way to see if they could find a topic that she couldn't use to talk about herself. They couldn't find one. He subscribed to the Hollywood dictum that an actor would set fire to his own mother for the chance of a good role.

He particularly loathed child actors—mostly for what their mothers had made them into. After a morning of watching children being interviewed for a part, he said he felt like going out and burning down an orphanage. He told us about a casting interview for the baby in a *Thin Man* sequel. The interviewer told the child's mother that he would have to work with Asta, who didn't like children, so it might be dangerous. No problem, she answered; that didn't worry her at all. Someone offered my sister (fifteen or sixteen and really beautiful) a bit role in a movie. My mother thought this was wonderful and asked if he couldn't find a part, "just a little one" for me. Papa was stony-faced. I knew it would never happen.

We went to hear Lena Horne in the Village (the first time I'd heard the F word used in public) and to "21," where we were seated next to an exhausted looking Tommy Manville and three aging blondes in satin décolletage. But it was the Stork Club that impressed me most—not for the food or glitzy service but for the other diners. This was the summer before the war reached America, and New York was filled with refugees, not the kind I'd seen in Pathé newsreels but slender, beautifully dressed women and men speaking French and languages I couldn't identify. Their features and their gestures were exotic to me. The women wore diamonds too large to be real, but you knew they were. Papa said something about the diamond merchants having fled Antwerp. He didn't seem especially interested. He was never impressed by European glamour.

I was uncomfortable in night clubs. They were smoky, crowded, and so noisy you couldn't really talk to anyone. You had to be a little drunk to enjoy them at all, I thought. I drank Shirley Temples. I don't remember about Mary. He drank scotch.

It was a mystery to me why Papa drank when it made him so miserable. If he had been a happy drunk, a "pints-all-around-at-the-pub" kind of drinker I might have seen some sense to it. But with Papa, though the evening might start out happily, it always ended badly.

When I was younger my bedtime prayer (really more of an incantation, because I believed as much in magic as religion) was that when I woke up in the morning God—or Somebody—would have taken away all the liquor in the world. I hated the stuff and the way it made people act. It made Papa and Mary senseless and unpredictable. Insane. I could see no difference between drunk and crazy. It turned my father maudlin or sarcastic-mean. Not violent; he was never that, and I was seldom the target of his sarcasm. But drunk he had a kind of lashing-out desperation about him that scared me to death. I couldn't understand how anyone so funny and kind could turn so awful; why a man who cared for his privacy and dignity so much could trash them.

This is a picture of Mary at about sixteen on the steps of the toyon house. I was surprised the first time I looked at a picture of her and realized how really beautiful she was. She could have made it in the movies or in modeling. Or she could have married what was known in Hollywood as a "rich millionaire." I've sometimes wondered whether it would have made any difference in her life if Mama had married again and we'd had a really strong, take-charge stepfather. Probably not.

Since then I've heard about all the usual explanations: His coming of age in the Prohibition and post-Prohibition times; that he moved in the drinking worlds in Hollywood and New York (spend a day with Nick and Nora and see what an incredible amount of liquor was poured down); that liquor is the great social lubricant. Papa was essentially shy, and drinking blunted that, making it easy to imagine himself as witty, urbane, and glamorous. That was its primary attraction for my sister, I think. In my daydreams I invented a sort of early camcorder that would follow Mary around in the evening so I could show her the next morning just how glamorous she'd really been. Then there was the hard fact of heredity. The Hammett family tree hung heavy with alcoholics. His own father drank. His brother. It was in the blood.

There's always the theory, especially concerning writers, of drink as anesthetic—that its use was to deaden their psychic pain. Well, Papa carried around a ton of that. But if he drank to deaden it, it sure didn't work.

What I believed as a child was that he drank to punish himself; when he was hurting others, he was hurting himself. That didn't, and still doesn't, make any sense to me. But maybe it makes as much sense as anything else.

The real mystery about Papa, though, was something else. He was wonderful enough when he was sober to make up for when he was not. That is saying an awful lot.

THE BEST PART of the summer was Hardscrabble Farm. People now seem to refer to it as Lillian's farm but Papa once told Mother that he and Lillian both put so much money into it that he didn't know what was whose. We always thought of it as their farm.

Hardscrabble was an hour-and-a-half drive north of the city in Westchester County and covered a hundred and thirty acres of mostly

A BAD ENEMY

Lillian liked to say, "I make a good friend and a bad enemy." I saw a beautiful example of Lillian in the latter mode during a nationally televised tribute to the composer Leonard Bernstein, who had clashed with her during their collaboration on Candide. *On the occasion of his birthday or some anniversary, various notables were giving testimony to his genius. When Lillian took the podium, beautifully dressed as always, she spoke eloquently for about five minutes—with not one word about Bernstein but a glowing and fond remembrance of his wife, who had recently died. It was perfectly Lillian—moving, apparently sincere, and, I have no doubt it properly skewered the maestro.*

wooded land. The original stone and white-frame house dated from before the Revolution. But that had been added on to and modernized. Lillian had put in a vegetable garden and had done a lot of landscaping. There was a stone barn, a guesthouse where Mary and I stayed, and another for the farmer who took care of the livestock and put in a couple of crops of alfalfa and corn each year. The house was roomy, comfortable and, like everything Lillian put her hand to, in flawless taste. She had brought her maid, cook, and driver up from the city. Lillian had definite guidelines for hiring servants. No elderly, she told me. They were too crabby. And no Jewish. They always wanted to give you advice. She seemed happiest with blacks.

She ran the house and kept an eagle eye on the staff. One night at dinner in the middle of a sentence she suddenly fell silent. When my father cocked an eyebrow at her, she said the driver was sneaking the car out of the driveway, on his way to spend an evening in town. I don't think he lasted long. The maid complained to me that Lillian insisted that she put fresh linen on every bed every day. I had to agree that it seemed excessive. At home Mother put a clean sheet on the top and the top sheet on the bottom once a week, something she'd learned in hospitals, I guess.

But Lillian could be kind too. She took an interest in the staff's personal lives, left a drink out on the sideboard for the repairman who came to fix the furnace. And when her Irish maid got engaged, Lillian offered to pay for the wedding—though later I heard her complaining to my father that she had never seen anyone in such a tizzy about getting married. "Maybe," Papa suggested with his faux-innocent look, "she's a virgin." "Oh, that's for certain," Lillian snorted. The way she said it, it didn't sound like a compliment.

Papa left the tedious domestic stuff to her. The servants loved him. "Mr. Hammett never asks for anything special," they said. He didn't have to. Somehow people were always trying to please him, to give him what he wanted before he asked for it. I'd noticed that before. It was some sort of trick he'd learned. Though I saw that it worked for him, I could never figure out how he did it.

Much of the entertaining was done at the back of the house out on a big sweep of lawn that was edged by the woods. A path on the left led off from it to the lake. The lake was where we spent most of our days. In the morning the farmer would hitch the brown and white pony (called Herman for Herman Shumlin, Lillian's longtime producer) to his cart and I would drive down to the lake. Papa and Mary would walk down, and we'd spend the day boating and fishing. Papa was endlessly patient with me, teaching me how to row and to paddle the canoe, untangling my fishing line from overhead branches and telling me my casting was improving.

Really it was. Though we did a lot of fishing, I don't remember actually catching anything.

It was at the lake where he was happiest, where he used to spend nights alone in the boathouse with one of the dogs for company. It held his guns and his fishing gear. It was the place where he seemed most at peace. I got up one morning just at dawn and walked down there by myself. There was a low mist over the water, just the tops of the two small islands rising through it. The tall trees all around as pale as smoke. It's a memory I've kept all these years. It must have been the one that he kept long after he'd gone to prison, they had lost the farm, and he was waiting to die.

MY FATHER AND I were at Lillian's apartment in New York in 1941, and Lillian was in the other room talking on the phone. When she came back, she was laughing. "I get the strangest phone calls," she said. This one had been from England: someone inquiring about the source of *The Children's Hour* plot. She explained, in an aside to me, that the play was based on an actual case involving a Scottish boarding school. Papa smiled, adding nothing, and that was the end of the discussion.

The incident meant nothing much to me at the time. I tucked it away as just another bit of evidence of the exciting literary life Lillian led. But as time passed, I learn a bit more about the writing of the play and its origins, and questions suggested themselves: Why hadn't Lillian taken the opportunity to acknowledge her debt to my father? We were alone; it would have been a kind and generous act, to him as well as to me. And why hadn't he said anything about his part in its discovery and development? It would have been only natural to take part of the credit. Why did they keep to their accustomed roles: she the accomplished author, and he the admiring, somewhat detached friend.

The scene took on a surreal, theatrical aspect. How, I asked myself, would the scene have played out in Bizarro World, the comic-strip universe where everyone is his own opposite, where up is down, black is white? In my mind I wrote the dialogue for the recast drama: Lillian, now painfully honest and warmhearted, comes into the room, explains about the phone call, and says to me, "You know, Josephine, it was really your pa who discovered the story, thought it would make a play, suggested it to me, and worked with me till I got it right." She beams fondly at my father who smiles back but, contrary to my written script, says nothing. I had given him a longish, rather cocky speech which begins, "Yeah, well I found the case in a book by William Roughead and right off I saw its possibilities. . . ."

It goes on to tell how he had thought of writing the play himself but then decided it was right up Lillian's alley, and how he'd held her nose to the grindstone till she'd gotten it right. But the words do not come out. He sits there mute, though still smiling, letting Lily have the stage, content to know what he knows, to have done what he's done. It seems even in Bizarro World Papa will not act against type.

MAN'S WORK

The things he seemed to take most pleasure in were working man's jobs, keeping his fishing gear in shape, refinishing a table for my mother. In the army when he was in charge of latrine-cleaning he would wait until just before inspection to get everything shiny wet and earn high praise for his superior efforts.

A DAUGHTER'S ATTITUDE

When my feeling and opinions went against my father, I usually kept them to myself. It was not a time when children—especially girl children—were expected to express themselves. And though Papa could sound like the most liberal free-thinker in the world, with his children he was not. There was a wide streak of Victorian father in him. I learned my lesson well: Do not tell adults things that may displease them. And never interrupt them when they explain yourself to you. It only upsets them.

PAPA'S ENLISTMENT IN the Army in 1942 came as a total surprise to us all. Even after he sent us his picture in uniform, I couldn't imagine him in the Army. None of my friends' fathers were in the service. A lot of them worked at Douglas Aircraft in Santa Monica, so they had exemptions. And they wouldn't have enlisted anyway. I was proud of Papa and got a kick out of surprising my teachers with the fact that my father was in the army.

Despite all the war coverage in the papers and radio, I didn't really worry about him at first. The war was far off and glamorous. Nobody I knew had actually been killed. I knew Mother worried a lot, but Mama worried about everything. It wasn't until a Saturday matinee at the Criterion that the war became real to me. A girl friend and I had gone to see a double feature—*Mrs. Miniver* and *Son of Fury*—and after the first feature, before the cartoon, they ran the newsreel: a company of Marines knee-deep in muddy water, slashing their way through a jungle somewhere in the South Pacific. I started to cry. The guys looked so miserable, so wet and dirty, and no older than the kids at my high school. It came to me that this was how the war was: nasty and dirty and dangerous. And that Papa might be in a place like that.

As I look back, his enlistment seems a cavalier thing for him to have done. He was forty-eight, with a history of serious health problems. On his best day he was only marginally fit. He'd had to persevere to find an army doctor who would attribute his underweight condition to his being a "rangy American type." In part his insistence on joining the military was an act of defiance against age, and decline, and sensible behavior. I think, too, that he'd felt bad about getting ill so soon after his enlistment in the First World War. He saw World War II as a chance to make up for it. Beyond these reasons, there was the simple fact that he wanted to serve his country. This was a just and necessary war, and he wanted to be part of it.

THE STRUGGLE FOR control of the Aleutian Islands began in June of 1942 with a Japanese attack on Dutch Harbor and the occupation of Kiska, seven hundred miles to the west. Air and sea skirmishes followed, and on August 30, U.S. Army forces went ashore at Adak. They expected to find Japanese entrenched there. But the only enemy was the hostile terrain and the bitter Aleutian weather. Within twelve days an airfield had been dug and that field, along with the one on Kamchatka, enabled U.S. forces to drive the Japs off Attu and Kiska at the far west of the chain. By the middle of August 1943 we were in control of the Aleutians and in striking distance of Japanese territories.

In 1944 my father, then a corporal in the Army Signal Corps, was assigned with another soldier, Robert Colodny, to write a history of the Battle of the Aleutians. He had come to Alaska in August of 1943 and, after some shifting around, ended up on Adak. His chief job was to edit the camp newspaper, *The Adakian*.

The Adak he knew was almost civilized. The troops had hot food,

Papa's enlistment in the Army came as a total shock to us. He was forty-eight and rail thin. It took him several tries before he could sweet-talk himself by the Army doctors. One of his early assignments was Fort Shenango in Pennsylvania, where the Army intended to keep potential "subversives" under a kind of house arrest. That ended when Eleanor Roosevelt found out about it and hit the roof. Papa had earlier met Mrs. Roosevelt and was impressed by her intelligence and humor.

On Adak in the mid-Aleutians Papa was assigned, along with another noncom, to write the story of the war there. He wrote it in a bare-knuckled, factual manner that expressed his deep admiration for the men who fought in that little appreciated, thoroughly miserable corner of the war. "The worst weather in the world," as meteorologists termed it, was as much an enemy as the Japanese. There were more suicides and breakdowns in the Aleutians than in any other theater of war. Papa was very happy there.

Quonset huts, movies, and warm showers. But there was still the biting cold, the sleet, and the Williwas, the fierce Arctic winds that could blow too strongly for the gauge to measure. So, when he sat down to write the history, it would have been easy for him to imagine how it must have been on Adak the year before: The men coming ashore, fully armed, expecting fanatical Japanese resistance, but with no tents, no protection from the wind, living off cold C-rations. They had dug into the hard island soil to shelter themselves the only way they could, in holes in the earth. They had unloaded a mountain of supplies and built the airfield, all in less than two weeks.

I can hear in Papa's writing the admiration he felt for those men, for their guts and determination. He thought American soldiers were as good as any anywhere. He was proud to tell their story and be a part of their army.

He goes on to tell the rest of the tale, the taking of Kiska and Attu. His tone and language sound brutal today. He used no euphemisms; he did not search for the politically correct phrase. The Japs were our enemy. We took pleasure in their being shot, blown up, bayoneted, annihilated. We might grudgingly admire their kamikaze spirit: that they tied bayonets to sticks when they had no rifles and killed their wounded so they wouldn't be captured. But we were at war; it was get them before they get you—a time to put aside humanity for survival.

IN MANY WAYS life on Adak agreed with my father. He developed a great affection for the men he served with. Most of them were young enough to be his sons.

The *Adakian* cartoons he sent home showed them as young, naive, endlessly pragmatic, short on everything but jokes and nerve. Probably

Papa wrote when he sent this shot that he thought he looked like "Foxy Grandpa." We weren't sure just who that was. He was called "Sam" or "Pop" by the other men, most of whom were young enough to be his kids. He managed to get through the heavy physical stuff by getting in a lot of sack time before and after. General Harry Thompson, who was in command of the area, was a mystery fan, and when he heard Papa was on Adak, he asked him to set up a camp newspaper.

they were much the same as the guys he had served with in the First World War. They called him Pop and told him their worries, chief of which was that being deprived of female companionship for so long a period would deprive them of virility. He told them that from his experience there would not be a problem. But his own celibacy was evidently not continuous. There was mention later on, in his cups, of an Indian woman and a bit of bad feeling with one of the guys. Details were not forthcoming.

On August 30, 1943, Papa wrote to Lillian, apparently describing this photograph: "Pictures, pictures, pictures! All he does is grow fat on the Army and send people pictures of the face. That's a bad sign on a man. Anyhow here they are. These were taken for Yank and they make me look like a Long Island clam digger who isn't doing so well against more vigorous competition. The garments, in case you can't place them, are fatigue clothes and arctic field jacket. They are our work clothes, but what am I doing?"

This is the shoulder patch worn by Army members in Alaska.

Joe Louis's visit to the Aleutians was an exciting event for the men there—especially for Papa who was a huge boxing fan and admired Louis tremendously. "He doesn't have a lot to say," Papa reported, "but he is far from being anybody's dope." Louis is sitting directly across from Papa, who is wearing his new sergeant's stripes.

In Anchorage, Papa invested in a night club run by Corrine Benny, shown here with Papa and Joe Louis on his visit. He fell off the wagon a few times but put most of his energy into the camp paper.

He liked his work with the paper and made it the best he could with news of the outside world, maps, and reports on the progress of the war. The action then was in Europe and the South Pacific. The men felt isolated and perhaps a little jealous of the guys in the midst of it.

He was fascinated by the Arctic landscape—its coastline, volcanoes, mountains. Alaska was stark, chillingly beautiful, nature at her most austere, out of bounds, gone too far. He loved about Alaska what he admired in people. Chance, and the U.S. Army, had landed my father in an almost perfect place. Adak, with its isolation, the rigor and limitation of its life, its cold beauty, suited him well. He was as happy there, or at least as contented, as he would ever be again.

Papa wrote the date on the back of this print: May 27, 1944, which would have been his fiftieth birthday. It looks like they are having a celebration in the *Adakian* office.

Here is the *Adakian* staff crammed into their meager quarters.

Papa told me this shot of the *Adakian* office was for publicity purposes and their real quarters was much less grand. He worked hard to get current war information for the paper—maps and news reports, magazines and papers. He wanted to keep the men up to date on the war and to give them a broad view of what was going on.

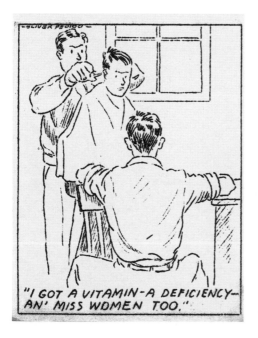

Papa sent home cartoons from *The Adakian* regularly and later on helped to get them published in a collection called *Wind Blown and Dripping*. He suggested some of the captions. I remember one line that seemed to summarize the necessary Adakian attitude. "You got to look on the bright side, even if there ain't one."

Early in my father's military career he turned over an army ambulance and never drove after that. During the Spanish Civil War there was some talk of his going as an ambulance driver for the Loyalists, but it was decided that he'd be more useful at home. I imagine a sigh of relief going up when he heard this— more from being spared the driving than the fighting. Though not a violent man, he would fight if he had to, as an op or a soldier. But he had no pretension about it being attractive or easy. In the forties he wrote me from the Aleutians, "I have not killed anyone. They will not let me." A very Hammett remark—funny, a bit shamefaced that he was not facing death with the men in Europe or the South Pacific, but also relieved that he was not directly causing anyone else's.

IT WAS 1944. Papa was in the Aleutians, and I was in my last year of high school. Papa had been in Alaska since summer 1943. His letters came more regularly than they had from New York. The Army had a schedule that he had to fit into—although it seemed a pretty loose one, as he talked about taking naps and going into breakfast whenever he felt like it. He sounded like he was enjoying himself.

In those days he wrote about equally to Mary and me, often including cartoons from *The Adakian*, the camp paper he edited. There was an occasional letter to Mama, asking for wool socks and the like. I always shared letters freely with my sister and mother, but there was one I did not.

In it he described two volcanoes that he had seen in this travels back and forth over the island chain. One was Shishaldin; the other was Pavlov. I went to look for them on the globe he'd given us that stood by the fireplace and found the Aleutians and Adak but no volcanoes. Papa described Shishaldin as the more showy and spectacular. The other, Pavlov, was quieter, steadier, less eye-catching. He liked them both, he wrote, but it was the smaller, less noticeable one he loved the most.

I put the letter in my algebra book, took it to school next morning and hid it in my locker. Mary frequently snooped through things at home, and I wanted to be sure neither she nor Mother saw it. I wish I could say that I hid the letter out of affection or compassion for Mary, but the truth is I knew there would be hell to pay if she read it and figured out what I thought Papa was saying: that my sister and I were the two volcanoes, and I was the one he loved the most.

At the end of the school year, clearing out my locker, I found that the letter had slipped through the cracks to the locker below and had been thrown away with the rest of the year's papers. I put it out of my mind until many years later, when reading a letter he had written Lillian at about the same time, I came across a mention of the volcanoes. This time there was no hint of loving anyone the least or the most.

By autumn of 1945 Papa was eager to return home. He was discharged in September at Fort Dix, New Jersey and went straight to the farm at Pleasantville. Despite the rather noncommittal tone of his letters to us, he came back with clear goals in mind: to be politically active, to organize, to teach and work toward what he believed in, perhaps even to run for pub-

JUST BEFORE THE MEETING STARTS! Dashiell Hammett, creator of "The Thin Man;" Doro
ker, writer and chairman of the evening; Mrs. Jerry J. O'Connell and Congressman O'Connell pa
a final word as they go onto the stage at Shrine Auditorium rally on Anti-Hitler Day.

Papa was active in left-wing causes in the forties. Before the war he worked with the Anti-Nazi League. In this photo from a newsclipping he sent home, he is on the way to one of their meetings. Dorothy Parker is on his left. After the war he worked with the Civil Rights Congress of New York. He was named its president in 1946 and helped organize protests against lynching, civil rights injustices, and voting abuses.

lic office. He had honed his organizational skills in the Army and was prepared to use them. He was named president of the Civil Rights Congress of New York. This leftist group was working actively for civil rights issues and freedom of speech. It frequently butted heads with the House Committee on Un-American Activities.

He began teaching, too—mystery writing and other classes at the Jefferson School of Social Science in the City. Teaching was perhaps the most surprising and valued talent he developed in his Army career. It was something he was good at and really enjoyed.

He had plans to get back to his own writing and started various projects, but other things kept interfering. Or perhaps he kept letting them

WOMEN

"I like women," my father told us once, partly to shock my mother, who looked away with a blush. "I really like women." It was true. He liked being around them; he was easy with them, sure of himself and his attraction. I think he mistrusted most men, kept his guard up with them.

interfere. In 1946 he brought my sister back to New York with him in hopes of getting her psychiatric help. He was beginning to see how really hopeless her situation was. Mary drank, and he drank with her. And he drank on his own.

Papa came out to California in July 1948 for my wedding. I had met Loyd Marshall when we were both in our junior year at UCLA. Loyd had flown with the Eighth Air Force in England and, after his discharge, had gone right into college, the first of his family to do so.

The Marshalls had had a cattle ranch and sawmill in Wyoming, but hard times and fierce winters forced them out. Loyd's parents moved first to Washington and then to California, where they settled in the seaside town of Santa Cruz. They were practical, grounded people, and I was pleased to be joining a family where rational behavior seemed the norm. And I was even happier to be acquiring a mother-in-law I liked and two sisters-in-law, whom I hoped would fill a gap in my life.

Papa was cold sober for my wedding celebration, very elegant in a dark blue suit as we walked down the aisle together. When I wrote him in New

York, nervous about telling him for the first time of my marriage plans, I asked if he would come out and give me away. "Give you away," he wrote back, very happy. "Why I'll drop you like a hot potato!"

He was at his charming best as I left on my honeymoon. But, two weeks later when I returned, he was as bad as I'd ever seen him.

Back in New York the drinking got even worse, and in December he was close to death. The doctors gave him a clear choice: Stop drinking or die. So he stopped, perhaps one of the bravest things he had ever done.

...

Loyd and I at our wedding reception on July 6, 1948 in the dining room of Mother's house. We left that evening for Santa Barbara and a honeymoon in Northern California. We both had just graduated from UCLA, and Loyd had a job waiting for him with the Navy at Pearl Harbor. I had a two weeks' wait before I could join him in Honolulu, so I came home for a few days. Papa was still there, but in a very, very bad way. I was glad to leave.

Papa and I in his bedroom at my mother's house on Purdue after my wedding. He'd slipped off during the reception, and I tracked him down. The photographer came in and took the photo almost before we knew it. Lillian had given me an antique blue and silver locket with the intent that I wear it on my wedding day. But I couldn't do that to Mother. I wore pearls instead.

Mother came over to visit us in Honolulu in spring 1949, and we did all the tourist stuff—went to luaus, toured the pineapple canning plant, and bought muumuus. Here we are by the Blow Hole on Oahu. Loyd flew in the National Guard and got to see the other islands. I stayed home, took hula lessons, tried to learn how to cook. We had signed on for two years, but there was a big reduction in force, so we came home in October 1949. It was a rough crossing, and I was sea-sick for the first time—probably being pregnant didn't help.

I GUESS I have to explain about Mary. She was four and a half when I was born and had whooping cough, a disease that can be fatal to newborns, so I had to be isolated from her. I suppose it's best not to make too much of that.

In her baby pictures, and there are dozens taken on the Eddy Street roof, she is a really pretty toddler, blonde, and, like Mother, blue-eyed. But she was trouble from the start. She threw Mother's nursing mementos into the gutter, slugged a nun at the Catholic school, shoplifted from the candy store (taking me along because I had handy bloomers for hiding things), cut school. She would lie even when the truth would have done just as well. And there was always trouble with boys.

She grew into a beautiful girl—Lillian said that at sixteen she was one of the most beautiful she had ever seen—and the house was always full of boys. In the beginning they were regular neighborhood kids, but soon they became older and more scary. The one she stuck with longest had a section-eight discharge from the army. Her drinking started early, and by fourteen she was a full-blown alcoholic. Later on there were pills.

Mother coped as well as she could, made excuses, cleaned up her messes, threatened, pleaded, prayed. Deeply ashamed, she did what our family always did with a problem: kept it to herself. I think my father had little sense that anything was really wrong with Mary before the summer of 1941 when she and I went east for a month-long visit. Mary was nineteen. Although my father kept his drinking to a minimum, one afternoon in the hotel, they both went at it. (I, loathing drunks even then, took myself into the bedroom and closed the door.) I learned later that she had told him all about herself and men. I imagine she sort of bragged about it, thinking he'd understand, admire her daring and to-hell-with-bourgeoise-morality spirit. Of course, he didn't. He was terribly hurt. What she never understood was that although he might have lived that kind of life himself, he never approved of it, even for himself, and certainly not for his daughter.

Five years later, after the war, Mother did the unthinkable. She wrote my father that she was desperate because Mary's condition was so bad. Could he come and help? He came at once, saw how bad things were, and considered taking her east with him where he could get her the best care.

I could see he didn't want to. When he asked me what he ought to do, I couldn't answer him directly. I looked away and said something about her thinking being twisted. What I didn't say was that it wouldn't do any good to take her east or get her the best shrink available. Nothing would help her. I knew I was fudging, but all I could think at the time was, yes, please, take her away and give Mother and me a little peace. I've had her for

Papa and Mary did a lot of drinking together after she went east with him in 1946. Here they are at Nick's in the Village. He'd brought her back to New York in the hope of finding good psychiatric help for her. He tried, but all that happened was that they both got worse. He was so bad in December 1948 that the doctors told him to quit drinking or prepare to die. He quit. But with Mary there was no such resolution; instead, she moved from liquor to pills.

twenty years. You take her for a while. I still feel guilty about that. Lillian understood. In the fifties, she said to me, "Don't feel bad about not being able to do anything for Mary. Nobody could."

He took her east with him and arranged for professional help. She was there off and on for five years. Then his other problems became overwhelming, and he asked the current shrink for an opinion. "There's nothing more we can do for her at this time," he was told. Those were bad years for both Mary and my father. Lillian told him his drinking set a bad example for Mary—as if she ever needed any bad examples. Of course, in a way he was an example. But what can you say about someone who copies only the bad and can't see all the good? She came back to Los Angeles in 1951 and stayed with Mother for the rest of her life. Nothing got any better. By that time I was married and had a home of my own.

WHEN I FIRST met Dotty Parker—in the forties, dinner at The Plaza in New York, I think—my father asked me what I thought about her. "Affected," I said, probably showing off a new word, and he snapped back that that was no way to talk about Dotty—I can't remember what word he used about her. Maybe sweet, though that doesn't sound like him. I got the message anyway: she was one of his own and you don't talk about your own behind their backs—at least to an outsider, which I was.

"So," I thought, "why did you ask me?" and absorbed another lesson in not telling people what they ask but what they want to hear. He'd asked me the same question years before about Lillian, but I had been smarter then and said, "Oh sure, I like her." Actually I didn't dislike Lillian as a child, but she scared the heck out of me. Even then, though, I realized that Lillian was too smart to ever be mean to me.

I didn't have any special feelings about Dotty Parker. She was kind toward me, rather quiet, not the great storyteller the others were. She was small and rather rumpled-looking, her eyes looked moist, as if she had just been crying or was about to start. I always picture her with a damp handkerchief in her hand.

I had heard Parker stories for years before that: about Dotty, going off to Europe to recover from some romantic disaster—her friends were always collecting money for her to get away—and she, standing at the rail, waving goodbye, saying, "I guess I put all my eggs in the wrong bastard." In their world that kind of wit made up for lots of other faults.

Much later I heard another version of that story—one which involved Dotty having an abortion, an unmentionable subject in those days. I wondered if Papa had cleaned up the true version for his little daughters. I would never have imagined then that anything he said had been cleaned up. But now I think it must have been. The Victorian papa peeked out once in a while when something really raunchy came up—like his squeamishness about a popular blues song called something like "I want some seafood, Mama." It took me years to figure that one out.

The bad feeling between my father and Dorothy Parker was largely one of Lillian's embroideries. As with Lillian's other dramatic fictions it served several purposes. It showed my father as sensitive and high-moraled in his reaction to Dotty's two-faced treatment of people. It showed Lillian as more tolerant and benevolent, and demonstrated how she suffered from his growing reclusiveness.

There was some truth in all these qualities. He did dislike Dotty's hypocrisy—the way she could be sweet as sugar to your face and then absolutely vile behind your back. Lillian was probably more tolerant of these foibles—at least when they didn't affect her. She was much more outgoing and in need of company than my dad. On my last visit with him on

This is a shot from 1938 taken at Tavern Island off the Connecticut coast. Whenever he could Papa would get away from the crowd. I think he had only a brief tolerance for people and needed to recharge in solitude. He liked Key West, too. He sat through a hurricane there all by himself, and he enjoyed it.

Martha's Vineyard one of the few things she complained about was that she missed having people in. Not that he would ever make a fuss about it. He'd just disappear into his room. He had always been a loner, and that tendency intensified as he got older. What my mother had first noticed about him at the army hospital was that he kept himself apart from the other boys.

For him, being around people could be difficult. He was shy and introverted. When my sister, in the forties, begged him to meet one of her friends—a particularly strange girl and the first lesbian I'd ever met—he said he'd rather not, that he had to meet so many people, as if that were the hardest part of being famous.

But he was inconsistent in that as in many things. In 1948, just after my marriage, I was home briefly waiting to join my husband in Hawaii, where he'd gone to work for the Navy. Papa looked Dorothy Parker up, and we all went to dinner at Chasen's—Dotty, Ross Evans (a stand-in for Alan Campbell, her ex), and another Hollywood couple. Dotty and Papa seemed on perfectly good terms—more of a credit to her, I would say, as he had been drinking and was generally unpleasant.

At the table he began flirting with the acquaintance's wife. I was sitting between them, and he acted as if I didn't exist. In a unique display of independence I got up as if to go to the ladies' room, leaving behind a new and expensive coat, sent a note back to the table, and got a cab home. My mother found me collapsed on my bed in tears. I didn't give her any details but sobbed out, "How could you have married a man like that?" She said, "He wasn't like that when I married him."

I was worried sick that he would be angry with me when he got home. But then next day when he strolled in, my coat over his arm, he was stone sober and very ashamed. "Was I pretty bad last night?" he asked. "Yes. You were awful," I said. We never mentioned it again.

...

PAPA MET PAT Neal in 1946, when she was cast as the younger Regina in *Another Part Of The Forest.* She was in her early twenties (my age almost exactly), just out of Northwestern and an overnight smash in Lillian's play. I first met her in 1950 in L.A. when my father brought her by to see my daughter Ann just after she was born. Pat was tall and beautiful. She seemed to realize it but not give it much importance. There was an openness about her—no showbiz glitz—and a vulnerability. She had had an affair with actor Victor Jory, who was twenty-four years older than she, which everyone brushed aside as a result of her youth. Later on she confided in Papa about her affair with Gary Cooper. ("I don't know much about him; never heard him say more that "nope" or "yup," Papa told me.) He and Pat stayed friends for the rest of his life. He loved her, and I suppose she returned some kind of love that was more like a daughter's than anything else.

Lillian saw it all and was hurt, though she tried not to show it. She called Pat "the starlet" and put on a tolerant, sardonic air. But the contrast must have been painful. Pat was strikingly pretty. Lillian, never beautiful to begin with, was aging badly. She had smoker's wrinkles and a sagging figure.

I always thought Lillian was attractive. She had such vitality and energy and intelligence. She carried herself as if she were a beautiful woman and wore elegant, expensive clothes. (Surprisingly once on Martha's Vineyard when I admired a handsome camel-hair coat, she told me a friend had gotten it for her wholesale. I shouldn't have been surprised. Lillian was always very smart with money.)

My father, in theory, scoffed at the importance of physical beauty in women. Looking at the cover of some pulp bodice-ripper he said, "Oh yeah, one of those books where the man is ready to give up the kingdom

This is Pat Neal at about the time my father met her, when she played the part of Regina Hubbard in the 1946 production of *Another Part of the Forest*. Lillian tried directing for the first time and drove the cast and crew up the wall. The only exception was Pat Neal, who got along beautifully with her. The play was only a moderate success, but Pat was a huge hit. She met my father at a rehearsal.

because some gal has a great set of tits." But with Pat it went beyond just great looks. She was so self-assured about it. Once when they were dining out he noticed that she had a nasty raw spot on her lip from an accident with a cigarette. Any other woman would have been mortified and tried to cover it up. But not Pat. She didn't even notice. She was lovely to look at, and no little blotch could change that.

He was not totally blind about her, however. "She's not the brightest kid in the world," he told me. He was lukewarm about her performance in the revival of *The Children's Hour* and pessimistic about her marriage to Roald Dahl. "A very silly, dull fellow." He told me he was glad she was getting a hefty diamond ring (described in Walter Winchell's column) out of it because she wasn't getting much else. She pleased Papa by promising to name her first born "Neal Dashiell"—which he said was the kind of a rhyming name that would appeal to her hillbilly mind. In fact her first child born in 1955, was named Olivia.

Papa was in Lenox Hill Hospital, very ill, at the time her son Theo was admitted with terrible head injuries. I hope he was past understanding when she visited him there. He was dead before her other tragedies struck—the death of Olivia from measles the year after his death and Pat's debilitating stroke. For this I am grateful.

PAPA WAS GAGA about Ann. She was born May 24, 1950 on my twenty-fourth birthday and three days before Papa turned fifty-six. When he flew out two weeks later, he held and looked at her as if she were the first baby he had ever seen. He took us to a lavish baby boutique in Beverly Hills to buy clothes and for lunch in his suite at the Beverly Wilshire. He was ecstatic.

The following spring he was out again, and we hatched a plan: He would fly east with Ann, and I would follow in ten days, stay on another

I have had a lifelong intolerance for people who must have everything spelled out or who try to put into words what can't be expressed. My mind goes back to an evening in the fifties at Lillian's brownstone. We were in the living room waiting for dinner and someone told the story of his neighbor who backed his car over his small son and killed him. There was a general murmuring of "Oh, no," and "How awful." When I looked sideways at my father, his head was down, his eyes lowered. And he was silent. Some things are beyond words.

week, and bring her home. I was not unhappy with the idea. As a nervous and exhausted new mother, I welcomed a quiet week at home. Loyd didn't object. It sounded like a chance for us all to get rested up.

Papa's flight east with Ann went well. She was an easy baby and slept the whole way. They had arranged for a nurse to come in (but had to bring in a substitute when the original one tripped and broke her ankle). When I arrived Ann seemed in fine shape. She had completely bonded with Papa. When I tried to take her from him, she turned her head away, which miffed me a little but pleased Papa immensely. She hadn't lost her

California tan, and with her rosy cheeks and blonde hair she made the eastern babies we saw look anemic. Papa said she looked like one of those Russian kids they liked to take pictures of sitting on top of a tractor. The nurse was competent, if, I thought, a little impersonal, and pleased me by telling Lillian that I was a "sensible young mother," implying that in her work she met lots who weren't.

Lillian left the physical care of the baby to Papa and the nurse, but she seemed genuinely delighted with her. It was a lovely visit. We passed our days on the lawn, Ann in her playpen, where visitors were expected to comment on her extraordinary qualities, or picnicking down by the lake. I had no cooking or cleaning to do. And the best part of all was Papa: not one drink passed his lips.

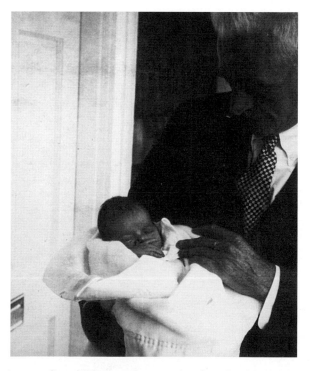

Papa came west when my first child was only a couple of weeks old, and my husband took this shot of him holding her. Papa fell madly in love with Ann, thought she was the most wonderful baby he had ever seen. He liked her name too. She was called "Ann" for his mother, Annie Bond Dashiell, and Marie for my husband's mother, Dollie Marie Jensen. He bought her a Steiff kangaroo with a baby kangaroo in its pouch and a ton of expensive baby clothes.

Papa taught evenings at the Jefferson School of Social Science in New York. He had discovered an aptitude for teaching during his army duties, and this Marxist college gave him the opportunity to instruct in his own field: the mystery. He was a rather laid-back teacher, disinclined toward any sharp criticism. Maybe he'd learned from his own experience that what writers needed most was encouragement and a sympathetic ear.

268. MYSTERY STORY WRITING

Dashiell Hammett   Thursday 6:45-8:15 P.M.

Fee: $12.00

A practical course in the writing of mystery stories, designed both for those who have worked in the field and for beginners. Problems of structure, mood and characterization are analyzed in terms of concrete work submitted by students.

269. WRITING PEOPLE'S POETRY

Aaron Kramer   Wednesday 6:45-8:15 P.M.

A workshop in the production of working-class poetry. Based on the rich traditions of poetry in many lands, from ancient times to the present. Major emphasis on group analysis and criticism of original poems by members of the class.

270. IMPROVING YOUR ENGLISH

Ethel Takce   Tuesday 6:30-8:00 P.M.

A course on the fundamentals of English grammar and composition. Designed to help progressives learn to write effective letters, resolutions, reports, etc. Emphasis on the practice of clear, logical and skillful writing on present-day subjects.

272. INCREASING YOUR VOCABULARY

Ethel Takce   Wednesday 6:45-8:15 P.M.

A course for the average reader or prospective writer who wishes to enlarge his vocabulary. Emphasis on the use of unfamiliar words for which there is current need, correct spelling, and precise distinctions between synonyms. Practice in the use of the dictionary. The study of word roots, and of the sources and development of the American language.

31

These are pages from the 1950 course catalogue for the Jeff School, as it was called.

Mother with Ann in late 1950. I had a willing baby-sitter in Mama. She was crazy about babies and extra crazy about Ann. I wish I had been as patient with my kids as she was. Shortly after this she had to go back to work. The Red Scare was in full bloom, and Papa lost his radio shows. His money was running out.

IN PRISON THEY told Papa he could only write to his family and lawyer, Charles Haydon. The family was Mother, my sister, and I. Initially, at least, Lillian had her letters returned. Mother and Mary wrote him often after he was moved to Ashland, but as far as I know I was the only one he answered. Those letters contain almost all he ever told me about being in prison. Later on if I asked him something, he would tell me, but he never volunteered. He was like that about the bad stuff—talking only made it worse. Not talking was how he got by.

He was sentenced July 9, 1951 on a charge of Contempt of Court. As trustee and chairman of a bail fund organized by the Civil Rights Congress, he had been subpoened to testify. The Court argued that he, and maybe some of the bail fund contributors, knew the location of four men convicted under the Smith Act who had failed to appear for sentencing, forfeiting their bail. As a witness, he was obligated under the law to make full disclosure. Following his attorney's advice Papa argued that disclosure would violate his rights under the Fifth Amendment, because it might make him subject to prosecution under the Smith Act. He believed, in addition, that his rights under the First Amendment were at risk: free speech, which included his right to keep silent. There was no doubt about the seriousness of the situation. The prosecutor was U.S. District Attorney Irving Saypol, who had prosecuted the Rosenbergs. Frederick Vanderbilt Field, another bail-fund trustee, had already refused to cooperate and was serving time. Papa refused to testify, too.

United States Second District Court Judge Sylvester Ryan sentenced Papa to six months in jail "or until he purged himself of contempt." Fat chance, I thought, knowing that "purging" wasn't an option for Papa, that his decision had been no decision at all. Papa had lots of faults, God knows, buckets of faults, but ratting on people who trusted him with their money and names wasn't one of them. Everyone said the real reason the feds wanted the information about the bail fund was so that they could get at the donors. It was 1951, the height of the Red Scare, and people were losing their careers, their livelihoods, and their reputations. Even when there was just a hint or accusation of being communists, their lives were shot. Papa had already lost his radio shows, *The Adventures of the Thin Man, The Adventures of Sam Spade,* and *The Fat Man,* at that time the main sources of his income. Anybody he named was in for what Lillian liked to call "bad trouble."

He would tell me later that he hadn't known where the fugitives were or even who the donors were. (A rather slapdash fund chairman, I'd thought.) Maybe if he had explained that to the court it would have gotten him off the hook, though probably not; they would just have thought he was weaseling. Or he might have done what Lillian urged: offer to testify about himself, but refuse to talk about the others. She used that ploy the next year in front of the House Committee on Un-American Activities and walked away without an indictment. Anyway, I knew there'd been no big soul-searching moral debate about whether he should fink or not. He'd done the only thing he could. And he wasn't feeling noble about it. He hated "noble." Later on he would sneer at Howard Fast, who was sweating out a possible jail sentence, for "groaning under a crown of thorns." If he'd been younger, in better health, you might have thought there was some macho, thumb-your-nose at 'em thing about it. But that had never been his style. It was the kind of BS he hated most in guys like Hemingway. He just did what he had to do, and the less said about it the better. He quoted the old cons—"You could do six months with your shoes on"—as if he believed it. He didn't, of course; he knew better.

They took him that afternoon to the Federal House of Detention on West Street in New York. Judge Learned Hand at first ordered $10,000 bail but then revoked the order after a petition by Saypol. Despite all later legal finagling he would never be permitted bail. In September they moved him to the Federal Correctional Institute near Ashland, Kentucky. But it wasn't until the middle of October that I got my first letter. I'm not sure why he took so long to write. I know he was sick and exhausted when he arrived at Ashland. He'd fainted in the food line. Maybe it took him those weeks to recover a bit and settle in to the routine. Or maybe he had to nerve himself up to write me. Even when you know you've done the right thing, the only thing, it would be hard to write your child from prison.

There was nothing romantic about it. Prison was claustral and demeaning,

How'll It Come Out?

Ace mystery fictioneer Dashiel Hammett (left), one of principal characters in The Case of the Red Bail Gold Mine, wrote this one, too, will have to figure out an ending. He is seen handcuffed to W. Alpheus Hunton, fellow big shot in Civil Rights Congress, on way to jail. Both were sentenced to six months for refusing to reveal where Communists get all that money, money for big time ball.

Dashiell Hammett Jailed For 6 Months in Red Case

Morris Warman

Dashiell Hammett leaving court last night on way to jail

DASHIELL HAMMETT JAILED IN CONTEMPT

Mystery Writer Gets Six Months on Refusal to Tell Where Communists Get Bail Money

NEW YORK, July 9 (AP)—M: mett drew a six-month prison tell where the Communist Par

A fellow bigwig in the Civil Rights Congress, W. Alphaeus Hunton, got a similar sentence.

U.S. Judge Sylvester J. Ryan sentenced both men for contempt, holding that their stubborn silence may aid the escape of four fugitive Communist leaders.

Linked to Red Fronts

Hammett in the past has been linked in testimony before a Senate subcommittee with 40 to 50 so-called Communist-front groups.

The sentences were the heaviest handed out by Judge Ryan since he demanded that Civil Rights officials reveal where they got the money to post $80,000 bail for the runaway Red leaders.

Last Friday Judge Ryan sent Millionaire Leftist Frederick Vanderbilt Field to prison for 90 days on the same charge.

Field spent the week end in jail but finally got out today on $10,000 bond. He is appealing a 90-day contempt sentence from Judge Ryan.

Large Bail Fund

The four fugitive Communists failed to show up for sentencing last week. A nationwide hunt is on for them. Their $80,000 bail—posted by the Civil Rights Congress—was ordered forfeited.

Judge Ryan insists the government might catch the four fugitives quicker if it knew who provided the Civil Rights Congress with the bail money.

The congress has a huge bail fund which it says comes from many contributors. The congress put up a total of $260,000 when all 11 Communist leaders first were released.

Hammett is chairman of the congress' bail fund.

Papa and was sentenced to six months in jail for contempt of court for refusing to answer questions put to him by the federal district court judge. What the court wanted, he felt, was not so much the whereabouts of the missing defendants, as the names of the contributors to the bail bond fund. He told me he didn't know either. These clippings were sent to us from New York, probably by Papa's secretary, Muriel Alexander.

as it was meant to be. The claustral part was not good. He'd suffered from that phobia all his life, though few people knew it. He hated small places, elevators, airplane cabins. I don't know how large his cell was. Maybe having bars to see through helped. But it was being cut off from his world that bothered him most, being forbidden to correspond with the two people who were most in touch with his affairs—Lillian and his secretary, Muriel Alexander. He asked me to ferry messages for him, and I did it as best I could.

In Lillian's case it wasn't easy. She had left almost immediately after the trial for Europe. I could tell he was surprised and hurt. But not angry. At least I didn't hear it in his voice. When he wrote that he'd heard "She seems to be having a pretty good time despite her worrying," I didn't detect any of what I would have expected—heavy-duty irony—only a kind of understanding wistfullness. "Well, that's Lily." I supposed she had reasoned that since she wasn't allowed to see or write to him, she might just as well be out of the country. I could understand that, but what was really shabby was the note she later fabricated from my father's lawyer as justification—purportedly relaying a message from Papa—ordering her not to come to the trial or try to see him and to go to Europe, "that you love so much." The whole thing sounded so much like Lillian and so unlike Papa that it would have been funny if you were in a laughing mood. Not one of Lillian's more credible creations.

No one at this time proved a better friend than Papa's secretary, Muriel Alexander. She visited him at West Street, tried to arrange bail money, ran errands. Muriel was to remain a true friend over the years, steadfastly guarding confidences, offering him companionship and, what he prized even more, silence when that was what was needed.

His message to Pat Neal, that he found it "awfully easy to be in love with her in jail," I found mightily embarrassing. I'd always felt a twinge of sympathy for Lillian where Pat was concerned. It seemed to me he had done nothing to conceal his attraction to her. Now he was sending her his love in the same paragraph as an inquiry about Lillian. It seemed disloyal, or at least indiscreet. I thought of Lillian as my father's wife. His marriage to my mother was history, and he and Lillian had been together as long as I could remember. Under any other circumstances he would never have shown his feelings openly like this. That he did told me just how alone and isolated he felt.

The *Los Angeles Times* carried the news of Papa's troubles in detail, and, of course, it was on the radio news. Walter Winchell was at his nastiest. But by and large people were kind. Many of our friends and neighbors didn't know who we were or simply ignored the whole thing. The exceptions were predictable—the idiot friend of my sister's who asked how I liked having a jailbird for a father, and my husband's Archie Bunker uncle, who gave me his More-American-Than-Thou speech. Nothing unexpected there.

1951 was a busy year for me. We had a new house, our first child, Ann (named for Annie Hammett), had been born the previous May, and I was expecting another in January. Papa was dotty about Ann. He'd bought me one of the new Polaroid cameras so I wouldn't have any excuse not to take pictures. I sent him dozens at Ashland. One of his few cheerful stories concerned the guard who gave him a picture of Ann in the buff just taking her first steps and said with a grin that ordinarily they didn't permit pictures of naked women, but in this case he guessed it was okay.

But this was a bad time for my mother. My dad had continued, as always, to support her and Mary. During the war years when we were about to lose our rental he'd bought Mama a little house in West L.A. Now his checks stopped coming, but there were still bills to pay, the house payments to make. She went back to nursing for the first time since her army days, getting on at St. John's in Santa Monica taking care of the newborns.

FRESH EYES

Papa liked gadgets. He had one of the first electric razors, a gold ballpoint pen (which he gave to me when I admired it), an early electric blanket. He admired the fresh idea—the idea that was perfectly obvious when you looked at it, except that no one ever had. Much of his genius lay in seeing the obvious with fresh eyes—that a man might really murder his own son as in The Glass Key, *that a married couple might have fun together as in* The Thin Man, *that a man might put other considerations above saving the life of his lover as in* The Maltese Falcon.

She loved babies and was wonderful with them; but the long hours were too much for her, and she was worn out with worry. I think Mother understood better than I did how hard prison would be on him. She had seen more of the rough side of life than I had, worked in the TB wards, seen men sick and dying. And she was less deceived by the tough-guy front he always wore. She knew his physical frailty, had nursed him in the San Francisco days when they both thought he was dying. She knew how much he needed his privacy and understood what its loss would mean to him.

The prison staffs didn't seem to be too hard on Papa. At the West Street center he worked in the library. In Ashland he did some mopping—Lillian said he was quite proud of his skill at cleaning toilets, but I think she was

From S D Hammett   12 Nov 51
PmB 8416, Ashland, Ky   (Date)
To Mrs Josephine Marshall   6531 W. 87th Place
(Name)   Los Angeles 45, Calif
(Address)

Dear Jo —

Thanks, honey, for the information about what we call business and stuff: with what dope I got from Haydon I think it fills me in pretty well and — unless, of course, something unexpected turns up (if anything turns up it will be unexpected) — I'll be OK until I get out of here in what seems like a very few short weeks --- The line in your letter about my "friend with the pearls" has me stumped though. Want to give me some additional clue? I'm probably a dope — it's probably not true that jail sentences sharpen the wits — but no amount of mulling has helped me guess whom you mean --- The weather this long week end has been quite wonderful and I've spent a bunk of both mornings and after- noons out in the yard, even though it's some- times better to pretend I don't hear the sounds of somebody in the nearby woods with a shot- gun --- Our lawyers had their chat with Supreme Court justice Jackson Friday, and Jackson, in turn, promised to repeat the chat to other members of the Supreme Court the next day to find out whether they wanted to hear us out — and that's how it stands now. We should hear how it comes out on Tuesday or wednesday. I've half a notion — write

At first when he was in jail, Papa was allowed to write only to his attorney and members of his family, which meant me, Mama, and Mary, so I ended up as intermediary. The problem was that only his secretary and Lillian really knew anything about his affairs. Lillian left right after the not much to base it on – that Fred may get out on bail while they listen to his tale of woe, and I may not. But we'll see ___ It doesn't make a great deal of difference to me whether I finish out my time now or go out on bail for a while and most likely have to come back and give 'em the three or four weeks I'll owe ___ Bed now and Gogol's "Dead Souls," a very funny book ___ Much of the nicest kind of love to you, sweetheart, and give my love to everybody, especially, of course, L and A –

Pop

SDHammett
8/16

sentencing for Europe. It seemed to be this isolation that bothered him most. But he didn't complain, even when his plea for bail was denied.

A Daughter Remembers   155

mixing up her stories. It was in the army that he bragged how well he shined latrines. He spent a lot of time in his bunk reading—Austen, Hugo, Gogol. He could always go to books when there was no place else to go.

They made him shave off his mustache, which he said he didn't mind (I didn't believe him), and he went back to using chewing tobacco, as he'd done as a kid. He said in a later interview that "prison made him feel like he was going home." Well, sort of. Maybe more like he was back in his Pinkerton's days—locked up in a Butte jail cell with some Wobbly he was trying to pump for information; rubbing shoulders with the same kind of rough guys the Anaconda miners had been—illiterate and stupid. But the inmates were tough, too, a quality he always admired, and often funny. He didn't look down on them, but he was not one of them either, although once he could pretend to be.

His feeling of being "home again" would have taken him back even farther than Pinkerton's days. In the woods around the prison he could hear the sound of hunters' guns, and his mind would have gone back to St. Mary's County and the woods around Hopewell and Aim farm, where he and his brother had fished and hunted. He loved the woods, knew all about animals, liked reading about them and watching them. Lillian said the only laws he was ever scrupulous about were fish-and-game regulations. He heard the guns outside the walls and wrote that he hoped to be out in time for a little duck hunting. But I guess it didn't work out; he never mentioned it again.

He was fifty-seven and his health, precarious when he went in, was going steadily downhill. He wrote vaguely of "being run-down," a euphemism he used to cover a multitude of ailments. He lost weight. When he was drinking or ill, Papa was almost a non-eater, and I imagine the prison fare was easy for him to ignore. He had grown used to good cooking— Lillian's, Chasen's in L.A., "21" in New York. He wrote longingly of the meal he had on order for his release: oysters on the half shell, quail, and sweetbreads. Papa was always heavy on the protein. "Feed the lettuce to the bunny and eat the bunny," was his theory.

There'd been an appeal to the Supreme Court with hope of early, at least temporary, release. But on December the fifth he heard on the prison radio that the Court had refused to hear his case. He finally got out on the ninth. They gave him fifty dollars' get-started money, and he took the Greyhound to Charleston. There he met a con he'd known inside. Papa gave him the fifty and got a flight to New York, where Lillian met him in a limo and took him home. Ten days later the U.S. District Court denied his second appeal, but by then it didn't matter. He'd done his time: twenty-two weeks, with thirty days off for good behavior.

I sent this picture of my son to Papa in March of 1952, when Evan was a couple of months old. Papa wrote that he looked as if he had everything in the world figured out. This was a hard year for us, with two babies in diapers and worry about Papa.

...

Papa GOT OUT of prison in December 1951 and went back to his old apartment in New York. It would have been smarter for him to lie low, given the political climate of the day, but instead he plunged right back into the battle, organizing and writing public statements of one sort or another. Much of this activity was directed against the Smith Act, which had been used as a means of jailing Communists.

His money situation was horrific. There was none coming in. His books had been taken off the shelves. His radio shows were blacklisted. The few royalties he would have received were attached by the IRS, which claimed he owed over $140,000 in back taxes. For the first time since their marriage in 1921, Papa could no longer support my mother.

And Senator McCarthy was not through with him yet. In March 1953 he summoned Papa to appear before the Senate Committee on Government Operations, which was looking into the use of federal funds to buy books by Communists for its State Department libraries abroad. Papa looked deathly pale, but he was never in better form. When McCarthy asked him if he would like to see the U.S. under a Communist government, he replied no; it wouldn't be practical if the people didn't want it. And when McCarthy asked if he himself would buy books by Communists for government libraries if he were in charge of fighting Communists, Papa answered thoughtfully that if he were in charge of fighting Communism, he wouldn't give the people any books at all. Chairman McCarthy seemed rather confused by that and dismissed him.

In February 1955 Papa went before a New York State legislative committee investigating charities, and, when asked about the Civil Rights Congress, which he still chaired, he said he didn't care if any of its mem-

This is Papa in the apartment he got on Tenth Street after leaving the army. It was near the Jefferson School and had an office downstairs, a fireplace, and a tiny garden, which I remember for its grimy ivy and soot-choked ferns. He wouldn't use the fireplace because he said he'd gotten to like the cold in Alaska.

bers were communists. That didn't matter to him. He only knew that CRC members were doing valuable work.

Perhaps his darkest time came in the spring of 1952, when Lillian, who had her own tax problems, was forced to sell Hardscrabble Farm. Home in bed with the flu the day of the moving-out, Papa wrote that its loss was going to leave a hole in his life and added wryly that Lillian suspected him of getting sick just to avoid the unpleasantness of the move. She might well have been right, I thought. But Papa always seemed to have people around him who cared. In the fall of 1952, when he could no longer afford to keep his New York apartment, Helen and Samuel Rosen offered the use of the cottage on their Katonah estate. Papa stayed there for five years. His health, never good after his stay in prison, went steadily downhill. In October 1955 he wrote that he had had a heart attack.

His letters came further and further apart. I wrote a couple of times, suggesting I come east for a visit, but he always put me off. Finally in 1960 it was clear that if I didn't go soon, it would be too late. Lillian had bought a house on Martha's Vineyard, where they spent much of their time. Loyd and I talked it over and decided to take a family vacation. We'd pack up the kids and go see Papa, whether he wanted it or not.

IN THE SPRING of 1960 my husband, who had kept up his Air Force flying skills, planned a cross-country flying trip. We took off from Ventura, California, in a four-seat Cessna, Loyd at the controls. I sat in the front next to him, the three children—Ann, ten; Evan, eight; and Julie, three—in the back. I was pregnant with Lynn, who would be born in September. We planned to stay a week on Martha's Vineyard, see my dad and Lillian, then head down the East Coast, visit friends in Atlanta and Biloxi, and fly home across Texas. Our first stop was Salt Lake City. For four and a half hours we were tossed around in the turbulent desert air like clothes in a dryer. Loyd had to give all his attention to managing the plane. The two older kids seemed to enjoy it; Julie went to sleep. Only I was miserable, too terrified to cry, too petrified to be sick. I held together by telling myself that when we landed I would go straight to the nearest Greyhound station and get a bus home. Loyd could continue on with the kids; I had to think of the baby and myself. But of course I didn't, and in Salt Lake we admired the statue to the sea gull and listened to the Morman Tabernacle Choir practice. The rest of the flight to Martha's Vineyard was relatively easy.

On the island we got a hearty welcome from the locals—the ferry to the mainland was on strike, and we had our pick of cars and housing. We settled on a cottage above the water, in a dense stretch of woods. We unpacked and I phoned Lillian. Her Mill House was in the village of

Vineyard Haven. It was a two-story house with gray shingles and white geraniums around the porch. My father had separate rooms in what was the original mill tower. Lillian later told me how little she paid for it, and I was amazed. To anyone used to southern California real estate prices it seemed like nothing.

Lillian was charming to the children and Loyd, whom she met for the first time. She seemed impressed by the trip—singling me out for praise as being very brave, because Loyd obviously enjoyed flying and the children didn't know any better.

My father was resting after a lung treatment. His emphysema was worsening. He'd had to stop smoking, although there was some kind of medicinal cigarette he used sparingly. I had trouble picturing him without a cigarette or pipe or cigar in his hand. My earliest memories of him all involve tobacco—silver cigarette cases, the cigar bands he gave me for rings, a lighter made like a revolver, the smoking jacket we gave him for Christmas, and the exotic aroma of Murads. When he finally came down to see us, he stopped for a moment, a dark silhouette in the doorway. As always I was surprised at how tall he was. My mind flashed back to my mother, five-foot-two, looking up at him after one of his long absences, and saying in wonder, "Sam, you're so tall." And him laughing down at her, "Well, I always was." Maybe I'm wrong about her calling him "Sam." If she did, it was the only time I heard her say it. He was always "Mr. Hammett" when she spoke about him.

He was nattily dressed, as ever—charcoal slacks and a sports coat, a paisley scarf at his neck, shoes a buffed cordovan. But he was so thin; it was almost as if he was not there inside the beautiful clothes. He moved slowly into the room, careful of what he was doing and gave me a brittle hug. Under the light his face was paper white and infinitely sad. He was pleased that we'd come, happy to see the children—Julie for the first time. I knew

I miss my father when:

Something funny happens, and I tell myself he would really have enjoyed that—he loved bits in the newspaper about people doing outrageous things. People going beyond what was the sensible, rational thing to do. People who didn't give a damn. He liked ridiculous names, funny (intentional or not) business signs, fractured English, jokes (dirty and clean), stories about show biz folk (usually salacious.)

I miss him when I read a really good book or see a play or movie and want to know what he would think of it.

I miss him when a political candidate makes a particularly inane remark, and I wonder just how Papa would have skewered him.

I miss him when one of my children or grandchildren does something great, and I want to tell him

What I regret:

I regret that I didn't ask him more questions: questions about his family; how it was in St. Mary's County growing up; about his mother and her family; about getting influenza; about his time in the hospital; about the Pinkerton's Agency. I excuse myself by saying he wasn't a man who seemed to welcome questions. Yet when I asked something he would tell me readily, though he wouldn't volunteer more than a direct answer. Occasionally he'd come up with some piece of the past on his own (One day in my mother's backyard, for no particular reason, he described the layout of the Hammett house in Baltimore: "You went through the kitchen, up the stairs and through the hall into my mother's room." The house and its rooms were fixed clearly in his memory. He could see it all as he spoke.

I regret that in one respect my father and I were too much alike. We both have a great natural reserve that makes it almost impossible to open ourselves to others. I think he would have liked to confide in me more, but I wasn't ready at that time to push for a more revealing relationship.

---

that he still loved us, but now it was in a muted, abstract way. Part of him was already gone. He had the look I would recognize in my mother's last days, a gaze turned inward. He'd already made the hard good-byes. It was painful to me, but comforting too, to know that the worst of loss was over.

We stayed for a week. The children played in the lagoon and romped with the poodles. Lillian took us on a drive around the island to see Gay Head and the lighthouse. Ann accidentally winged Evan with a rock, and he had to get stitches. I was not alone with my father much. He asked about Mother and Mary briefly but didn't pursue it. Then, in one sudden moment of revelation, he told me he tried to typewrite sometimes but his fingers wouldn't do what his brain told them; the letters came out wrong. I was numb. I reached into my handy Catholic grab-bag: "Well, I guess we all have our crosses to bear." I was appalled when I heard what had come out of my mouth. But strangely it was the right thing. He laughed, his old

These photos were taken on the steps of Lillian's Mill House, on Martha's Vineyard in the spring of 1960. This was to be the last time I saw my father, and we all knew it. Lynn, the granddaughter he never saw, would be born in September. Papa died in January 1961, and Lillian in 1984, outliving my husband by two years. "She's a funny old world," as Papa once put it. Loyd and I took the photos. In the top one Lillian is sitting next to Loyd. In the bottom one, my daughters Ann and Julie are sitting between me and Papa, and Evan is on my left.

Hammett self again, as if I had said something really brilliant. "Boy, how right you are," he said. We changed the subject after that.

I bumped into Lillian in the village, and we went for coffee. She told me that she suffered from the isolation imposed by my father. She liked making dinner for people, having friends in for coffee, chatting with tradesmen. She went briefly into my father's sorry financial situation and told me she would be his executrix. Her final remark on the subject was a cheerful, "We won't fight about money, will we."—Not really a question but a confident prediction.

She asked about Mary but listened without interest. She had written her off. I told her Mother was still working at St. John's Hospital in Santa Monica, but the work and the constant worry about Mary was hard for her. Lillian was not sympathetic. Mother should have remarried or gone back to work earlier, she felt. "She's made her own bed, and now she must sleep in it," she had once told me. Lillian could sound biblical on such occasions. Then she smiled at me and said, "You know it was never a real marriage— your father and your mother. It was over before it began."

"But," I protested, " My sister and I are almost five years apart. That's not so short—"

"Some day I'll tell you about it," Lillian said, sad but kind, with no hint yet of The Awful Secret.

She asked if I realized that my father was dying. I said yes. She told me that the doctors expected him to be much worse soon, too ill for her to care for. "He says he will go into a Veterans' hospital then. What do you think of that?" She told me not to answer right away, but think about it. I did, and a few days later told her that that was probably a sensible idea. "Sensible" had always been Lillian's highest word of praise for me. I was the "sensible one" in my family. I was a "sensible young mother" with Ann. I took it as a compliment then. I should have known better. She made no reply, and it was not until I was on the flight home that I realized what she was really asking: Since she would not be able to take care of him, would I? My formidable obtuseness must have been a sore trial for Lillian.

She complained about my father, but when I was with him I saw nothing but kindness and patience from her. On the last evening of our stay he was barbecuing on the outdoor grill with unsteady hands and let the steak fall into the ashes. It was a terrible moment. I was struck mute. I couldn't look at his face. But Lillian retrieved the meat quietly, made a little joke, brushed off the ashes, and they continued the meal preparation. In that moment I felt as close to her as I ever will. She had the burden of his care, didn't want it, but took it anyway. Much of what they had had together was gone—the fun, the sex, the fighting—but the love remained. I could be wrong about a lot of things with Lillian, but not about that.

We were scheduled to leave the next morning, but a dense fog settled over the island and the airfield was closed. I telephoned Lillian and agreed not to let my father know that we are still there. We had said our goodbyes, brief and dry-eyed, and neither of us could go through that again.

Once, a long time before, we were talking about suffering, and my father said, "People always say things like, 'Oh, well, he was suffering so much that he was better off dying.' But it's not true. You're always better off living." I wondered if he still felt that way?

I suppose he did.

It was a cool January morning in 1961 just after six. I was in the kitchen heating Lynn's bottle and hoping Julie would sleep in until I got the older kids off to school, when the phone rang. It was Lillian. "Your father's dead," she said.

"Oh, I'm so sorry," I said. "You've been through a terrible time, Lillian."

This is the last photo of Papa, so far as I know. He was sixty-six.

I was grateful that Lillian arranged for my father to be buried at Arlington. It's a beautiful site, up near the Tomb of the Unknown Soldier. She wanted me to get the inscription, "Samuel D. Hammett" changed to "Samuel Dashiell Hammett." But I think he would like it the way it is, the way it read on his dog tag.

"Yes," she said. "And I've had no help at all." She paused. "I suppose you're not coming for the funeral."

"We'll have to see."

I still feel bad about the funeral. I should have gone, could have gone. When people asked, I used Loyd and the kids—the baby was four months old—as an excuse, but they weren't the real reason.

Mama was already at work that morning at St. John's Hospital in Santa Monica. Mrs. Donagan from our old neighborhood, who always liked to be first with that kind of news, phoned her there: "Mr. Hammett is dead. It was on the radio." Poor Mama. She had no luck at all.

When I saw her the next day she seemed more tired than anything. She asked me about plans for the funeral and began talking about what clothes to take.

Mary and I were horrified. "It's not a good idea, your going. It's really not," we both told her. Mother looked at us bewildered: "But I'm the wife, she said—not "his wife" but "the wife."

Images of the funeral floated before my eyes: the drive to the cemetery, Mother sharing a car with Lillian. The small group hovering around the grave. Mother to one side, alone, shivering in her thin California clothes, crying, and no one to comfort her. Maybe a reception somewhere after. What would anyone say to her, or she to anyone? It would be horrible for her, and for everyone.

We kept telling her that going to the funeral wouldn't be a good idea until finally she saw it and for the first time broke down in tears.

So it was that none of us went east for the funeral. Mary, who in times of crises was capable of staying sober, sensibly didn't even offer. I thought I should go, but there were the kids to see to. Loyd couldn't take off work, and Mother, who frequently sat with them, didn't offer. I couldn't bring myself to ask—or to go to Papa's funeral when she couldn't.

Funerals are really for the living. There's not much you can do for the dear departed. Papa would have understood. He wasn't terribly punctilious himself. No, that's not what I really feel bad about. It's the years before when he was sick and broke and without solace. That's when I should have been with him and been a companion or at least a presence. Should have been and might have been if he had not chosen such a singular and solitary road to travel and we had not both walled ourselves into our separate silences.

SHORTLY AFTER MY mother died in November 1980, Lillian wrote me to confide what became known in my family as The Awful Secret—which was that my sister was in fact not my father's child, but the daughter of some other serviceman that Mother had a brief affair with. My father had known that she was pregnant and had married her out of a sort of chivalrous gallantry. It was a marriage in name only, over before it began. Lillian had kept this to herself while my mother was alive, but now she thought I had the right to know.

I was delighted and began—against instructions—to confide in my husband and children. It seemed heaven-sent—at least part of Mary was not related to me—the nutty part, I hoped. I went around elated for weeks before common sense reared its ugly head. My husband reminded me that this had all the earmarks of one of Lillian's Dramas of the Month and was a fine example of her creativity. She was a gifted creator of true-life events. Scenes that never happened were staged in realistic detail: "Don't you remember? We had just eaten lunch." "I have the clipping upstairs some-where." In this case, "I knew the soldier's name once, but I've forgotten it."

Lillian produced authentic dialogue: my father's mother, "This marriage will kill me." (Why she would be so upset by it, Lillian didn't say—when mother was the right color, religion, and a nurse as Annie Hammett had been.) Lillian threw in her own rational comment, "Well, of course, it didn't. She may not have liked it, but it didn't kill her." Actually Annie H. died the year my parents were married, 1921.

I came down off my rosy cloud and saw this for what it was—a prime example of Lillian re-writing life so it played better. A gifted storyteller, she was careful to keep action consistent with character—which was what had made this so convincing. It was the kind of gallant action my father was capable of, and the pay off would have been have been splendid for Lillian. It would have made my mother look promiscuous and my father look noble; it would have exed Mary, whom she detested (not without good reason) out of the family circle; and, perhaps most important, it would have added another note of high drama to the Hammett-Hellman mystique.

There is a line in one of Lillian's play's that I think explains a lot about its author: "God forgives those who invent what they need."

CODA

"So," PEOPLE ASK me, when the ice is broken, and they get to the thing they really want to know, the important thing: "Why did your father stop writing?" I can see Papa over their shoulders. One eyebrow goes up; he gives me his long-suffering-saint smile; and he settles down to listen patiently while I go down the list.

"Well, he drank you know," I begin. "And for a long time he had enough money so he didn't have to write. He could do other things, like politics and fishing. He wanted to go mainstream, but that was scary, because he'd been so successful with mysteries. Then there was the army. And his health was bad." I don't mention prison. He hates that.

But people aren't satisfied. "No, but really . . ." they insist. When I look back at Papa he gives me a what-can-you-do shrug. We both know what the trouble is. The answers are okay; it's the question that's wrong. He didn't stop writing. Not until the very last. What he stopped was finishing.

"Well, actually," I start again, "between 1938 and 1952 he began at least three different novels: 'My Brother Felix' (which became 'Toward Z' and then 'There Was a Young Man'), 'The Valley Sheep Are Fatter,' and 'Tulip.'" He must have finished large chunks of them, but only 25,000 words or so of "Tulip" have been found.

"He was enthusiastic beginning each new novel, though he wouldn't go into details. 'Don't ask me what it's about—about people, maybe,' he wrote Mary in 1938. But he had gotten out of the habit of steady work. Weeks and months were broken up with other things—other people's work—and when he got back to the book he was no longer so sure that it was a good idea, that he could bring it off. The trouble was he wanted to go main-stream. He wanted it badly. And maybe that—the wanting—worked against him.

"Because," I go on, "there was always the danger of actually finishing a book." People look at me blankly and I try to explain: "You know, when it's really finished, done, then it's set forever, and you can't fix it any more. You have to face the critics and yourself if it's bad.

"Of course, he had lots of ways of putting that off—football games, making fishing lures, drinking. And he could read forever. What he decid-ed in the end was that he was tired. He'd lived enough for half-a-dozen men. He'd said everything he wanted to say. It was time to shut up.

"He gives Pop, a character in 'Tulip,' his thoughts on that: 'If you are tired you ought to rest, and not try to fool yourself and your customers with colored bubbles.'

"It is that simple, nothing very complicated about it," I sum it up neatly.

I look back to where Papa is and mouth, "I'm sorry—as if you had ever done anything simple and uncomplicated in your whole life. And as if I could explain it if you had." But, as I might have expected, he's lost inter-est and wandered off.

People are disappointed. They were hoping for something more dra-matic, something insightful. Then they ask, more polite than interested: "So what's 'Tulip' about?"

"Well," I tell them, "there's this writer who's stopped writing, except he's writing a book about not writing."

They look at me, embarrassed. "Sorry," they say, "We don't quite get it . . ."

"Don't feel bad," I reassure them. "It's like what Pop says in 'Tulip': 'People almost never do.'"